ABOUT THIS PUBLICATION

FOR SERVICE ASSISTANCE

Customer Service
1.704.898.0770

North Carolina General Statues is published by The Muliti-Media Group of Greater Charlotte in Charlotte, North Carolina. Copyright 2015 by the Multi-Media Group of Greater Charlotte. This book or parts thereof may not be reproduced in any form, stored in a retrieval system, or transmitted in any form by any means—electronic, mechanical, photocopy, recording or otherwise—without prior written permission of the publisher, except as provided by United States of America copyright law.

The records required by U.S. Code 2257(a) through (c) and the pertinent regulations 28 C.F.R. Cli. 1, Part 75 with respect to this publication and all materials associated with such records are maintained by The Multi-Media Group of Greater Charlotte, Publisher and available for review by Attorney General.

www.visionbooks.org

Copyright © 2015 by MMGGC
All rights reserved!

TID: 5109360
ISBN (10) digit: 1503255034
ISBN (13) digit: 978-1503255036

123-4-56789-01239-Paperback
123-4-56789-01239-Hardback

First Edition

090520140547

Printed in the United States of America

2015 EDITION

North Carolina Criminal Law And Procedure-Pamphlet # 92

Printed In conjunction with the Administration of the Courts

North Carolina Criminal Law and Procedure
Pamphlet Reference Guide

Chapters	Pamphlet
Chapter 1 Civil Procedure	1
Chapter 1 Civil Procedure (Continue)	2
Chapter 1A Rules of Civil Procedure	2
Chapter 1B Contribution.	2
Chapter 1C Enforcement of Judgments.	2
Chapter 1D Punitive Damages.	2
Chapter 1E Eastern Band of Cherokee Indians.	2
Chapter 1F North Carolina Uniform Interstate Depositions and Discovery Act.	2
Chapter 2 - Clerk of Superior Court [Repealed and Transferred.]	3
Chapter 3 - Commissioners of Affidavits and Deeds [Repealed.]	3
Chapter 4 - Common Law	3
Chapter 5 - Contempt [Repealed.]	3
Chapter 5A - Contempt	3
Chapter 6 - Liability for Court Costs	3
Chapter 7 - Courts [Repealed and Transferred.]	3
Chapter 7A – Judicial Department	3
Chapter 7A – Continuation (Judicial Department)	4
Chapter 7A – Continuation (Judicial Department)	5
Chapter 7B - Juvenile Code	5
Chapter 8 - Evidence	6
Chapter 8A - Interpreters for Deaf Persons [Recodified.]	6
Chapter 8B - Interpreters for Deaf Persons	6
Chapter 8C - Evidence Code	6
Chapter 9 - Jurors	6
Chapter 10 - Notaries [Repealed.]	6
Chapter 10A - Notaries [Recodified.]	6
Chapter 10B - Notaries	6
Chapter 11 - Oaths	6
Chapter 12 - Statutory Construction	6
Chapter 13 - Citizenship Restored	6
Chapter 14 - Criminal Law	7
Chapter 14 –Criminal Law (Continuation)	8
Chapter 15 - Criminal Procedure	9
Chapter 15A - Criminal Procedure Act (Continuation)	10
Chapter 15A - Criminal Procedure Act (Continuation)	11
Chapter 15B - Victims Compensation	11
Chapter 15C - Address Confidentiality Program	11
Chapter 16 - Gaming Contracts and Futures	11
Chapter 17 - Habeas Corpus	11

Chapter	Page
Chapter 17A - Law-Enforcement Officers [Recodified.]	11
Chapter 17B - North Carolina Criminal Justice Education and Training System [Recodified.] Chapter 17C - North Carolina Criminal Justice Education and Training Standards Commission	11
Chapter 17D - North Carolina Justice Academy	11
Chapter 17E - North Carolina Sheriffs' Education and Training Standards Commission	11
Chapter 18 - Regulation of Intoxicating Liquors [Repealed.]	12
Chapter 18A - Regulation of Intoxicating Liquors [Repealed.]	12
Chapter 18B - Regulation of Alcoholic Beverages	12
Chapter 18C - North Carolina State Lottery	12
Chapter 19 - Offenses against Public Morals	12
Chapter 19A - Protection of Animals	12
Chapter 20 - Motor Vehicles	13
Chapter 20 - Motor Vehicles (Continuation)	14
Chapter 20 - Motor Vehicles (Continuation)	15
Chapter 20 - Motor Vehicles (Continuation)	16
Chapter 21 - Bills of Lading	17
Chapter 22 - Contracts Requiring Writing	17
Chapter 22A - Signatures	17
Chapter 22B - Contracts Against Public Policy	17
Chapter 22C - Payments to Subcontractors	17
Chapter 23 - Debtor and Creditor	17
Chapter 24 – Interest	17
Chapter 25 – Uniform Commercial Code	18
Chapter 25 – Uniform Commercial Code (Continuation)	19
Chapter 25A – Retail Installment Sales Act	20
Chapter 25B - Credit	20
Chapter 25C - Sales of Artwork	20
Chapter 26 - Suretyship	20
Chapter 27 - Warehouse Receipts [Repealed.]	20
Chapter 28 - Administration [Repealed.]	20
Chapter 28A - Administration of Decedents' Estates	20
Chapter 28B - Estates of Absentees in Military Service	20
Chapter 28C - Estates of Missing Persons	20
Chapter 29 - Intestate Succession	21
Chapter 30 - Surviving Spouses	21
Chapter 31 - Wills	21
Chapter 31A - Acts Barring Property Rights	21
Chapter 31B - Renunciation of Property and Renunciation of Fiduciary Powers Act	21
Chapter 31C - Uniform Disposition of Community Property Rights at Death Act	21
Chapter 32 - Fiduciaries	21
Chapter 32A - Powers of Attorney	21
Chapter 33 - Guardian and Ward [Repealed and Recodified.]	21

Chapter 33A - North Carolina Uniform Transfers to Minors Act	21
Chapter 33B - North Carolina Uniform Custodial Trust Act	21
Chapter 34 - Veterans' Guardianship Act	22
Chapter 35 - Sterilization Procedures	22
Chapter 35A - Incompetency and Guardianship	22
Chapter 36 - Trusts and Trustees [Repealed.]	22
Chapter 36A - Trusts and Trustees	22
Chapter 36B - Uniform Management of Institutional Funds Act [Repealed.]	22
Chapter 36C - North Carolina Uniform Trust Code	22
Chapter 36D - North Carolina Community Third Party Trusts, Pooled Trusts	23
Chapter 36E - Uniform Prudent Management of Institutional Funds Act	23
Chapter 37 - Allocation of Principal and Income [Repealed.]	23
Chapter 37A - Uniform Principal and Income Act	23
Chapter 38 - Boundaries	23
Chapter 38A - Landowner Liability	23
Chapter 39 - Conveyances	23
Chapter 39A - Transfer Fee Covenants Prohibited	23
Chapter 40 - Eminent Domain [Repealed.]	23
Chapter 40A - Eminent Domain	23
Chapter 41 - Estates	23
Chapter 41A - State Fair Housing Act	23
Chapter 42 - Landlord and Tenant	23
Chapter 42A - Vacation Rental Act	23
Chapter 43 - Land Registration	23
Chapter 44 - Liens	24
Chapter 44A - Statutory Liens and Charges	24
Chapter 45 - Mortgages and Deeds of Trust	24
Chapter 45A - Good Funds Settlement Act	24
Chapter 46 - Partition	24
Chapter 47 - Probate and Registration	25
Chapter 47A - Unit Ownership	25
Chapter 47B - Real Property Marketable Title Act	25
Chapter 47C - North Carolina Condominium Act	25
Chapter 47D - Notice of Settlement Act [Expired.]	25
Chapter 47E - Residential Property Disclosure Act	25
Chapter 47F - North Carolina Planned Community Act	25
Chapter 47G - Option to Purchase Contracts	25
Chapter 47H - Contracts for Deed	25
Chapter 48 - Adoptions	26
Chapter 48A - Minors	26
Chapter 49 - Bastardy	26
Chapter 49A - Rights of Children	26
Chapter 50 - Divorce and Alimony	26
Chapter 50A - Uniform Child-Custody Jurisdiction and	

Enforcement Act	26
Chapter 50B - Domestic Violence	26
Chapter 50C - Civil No-Contact Orders	26
Chapter 51 - Marriage	26
Chapter 52 - Powers and Liabilities of Married Persons	27
Chapter 52A - Uniform Reciprocal Enforcement of Support Act [Repealed.]	27
Chapter 52B - Uniform Premarital Agreement Act	27
Chapter 52C - Uniform Interstate Family Support Act	27
Chapter 53 - Banks	27
Chapter 53A - Business Development Corporations and North Carolina Capital Resource Corporations	28
Chapter 53B - Financial Privacy Act	28
Chapter 54 - Cooperative Organizations	28
Chapter 54A - Capital Stock Savings and Loan Associations [Repealed.]	28
Chapter 54B - Savings and Loan Associations	29
Chapter 54C - Savings Banks	29
Chapter 55 - North Carolina Business Corporation Act	30
Chapter 55A - North Carolina Nonprofit Corporation Act	31
Chapter 55B - Professional Corporation Act	31
Chapter 55C - Foreign Trade Zones	31
Chapter 55D - Filings, Names, and Registered Agents for Corporations, Nonprofit Corporations, and Partnerships	31
Chapter 56 - Electric, Telegraph and Power Companies [Repealed.]	31
Chapter 57 - Hospital, Medical and Dental Service Corporations [Recodified.]	31
Chapter 57A - Health Maintenance Organization Act [Recodified.]	31
Chapter 57B - Health Maintenance Organization Act [Recodified.]	31
Chapter 57C - North Carolina Limited Liability Company Act.	31
Chapter 58 - Insurance.	32
Chapter 58 - Insurance (Continuation)	33
Chapter 58 - Insurance (Continuation)	34
Chapter 58 - Insurance (Continuation)	35
Chapter 58 - Insurance (Continuation)	36
Chapter 58 - Insurance (Continuation)	37
Chapter 58 - Insurance (Continuation)	38
Chapter 58A - North Carolina Health Insurance Trust Commission [Recodified.]	38
Chapter 59 - Partnership.	39
Chapter 59B - Uniform Unincorporated Nonprofit Association Act.	39
Chapter 60 - Railroads and Other Carriers [Repealed and Transferred.]	39
Chapter 61 - Religious Societies	39
Chapter 62 - Public Utilities	39

Chapter 62 - Public Utilities (Continuation)	40
Chapter 62A - Public Safety Telephone Service And Wireless Telephone Service	40
Chapter 63 - Aeronautics	40
Chapter 63A - North Carolina Global TransPark Authority	40
Chapter 64 - Aliens	40
Chapter 65 – Cemeteries	40
Chapter 66 - Commerce and Business	41
Chapter 67 - Dogs	41
Chapter 68 - Fences and Stock Law	41
Chapter 69 - Fire Protection	41
Chapter 70 - Indian Antiquities, Archaeological Resources and Unmarked Human Skeletal Remains Protection	42
Chapter 71 - Indians [Repealed.]	42
Chapter 71A - Indians	42
Chapter 72 - Inns, Hotels and Restaurants	42
Chapter 73 - Mills	42
Chapter 74 - Mines and Quarries	42
Chapter 74A - Company Police [Repealed.]	42
Chapter 74B - Private Protective Services Act [Repealed.]	42
Chapter 74C - Private Protective Services	42
Chapter 74D - Alarm Systems	42
Chapter 74E - Company Police Act	42
Chapter 74F - Locksmith Licensing Act	42
Chapter 74G - Campus Police Act	42
Chapter 75 - Monopolies, Trusts and Consumer Protection	42
Chapter 75A - Boating and Water Safety	43
Chapter 75B - Discrimination in Business	43
Chapter 75C - Motion Picture Fair Competition Act	43
Chapter 75D - Racketeer Influenced and Corrupt Organizations	43
Chapter 75E - Unlawful Activities in Connection With Certain Corporate Transactions	43
Chapter 76 - Navigation	43
Chapter 76A - Navigation and Pilotage Commissions	43
Chapter 77 - Rivers, Creeks, and Coastal Waters	43
Chapter 78 - Securities Law [Repealed.]	43
Chapter 78A - North Carolina Securities Act	43
Chapter 78B - Tender Offer Disclosure Act [Repealed.]	43
Chapter 78C - Investment Advisers	43
Chapter 78D - Commodities Act	43
Chapter 79 - Strays [Repealed.]	43
Chapter 80 - Trademarks, Brands, etc.	44
Chapter 81 - Weights and Measures [Recodified.]	44
Chapter 81A - Weights and Measures Act of 1975.	44
Chapter 82 - Wrecks [Repealed.]	44
Chapter 83 - Architects [Recodified.]	44

Chapter 83A - Architects	44
Chapter 84 - Attorneys-at-Law	44
Chapter 84A - Foreign Legal Consultants	44
Chapter 85 - Auctions and Auctioneers [Repealed.]	44
Chapter 85A - Bail Bondsmen and Runners [Recodified.]	44
Chapter 85B - Auctions and Auctioneers	44
Chapter 85C - Bail Bondsmen and Runners [Recodified.]	44
Chapter 86 - Barbers [Recodified.]	44
Chapter 86A - Barbers	44
Chapter 87 - Contractors	44
Chapter 88 - Cosmetic Art [Repealed.]	44
Chapter 88A - Electrolysis Practice Act	44
Chapter 88B - Cosmetic Art	45
Chapter 89 - Engineering and Land Surveying [Recodified.]	45
Chapter 89A - Landscape Architects	45
Chapter 89B - Foresters	45
Chapter 89C - Engineering and Land Surveying	45
Chapter 89D - Landscape Contractors	45
Chapter 89E - Geologists Licensing Act	45
Chapter 89F - North Carolina Soil Scientist Licensing Act	45
Chapter 89G - Irrigation Contractors	45
Chapter 90 - Medicine and Allied Occupations	45
Chapter 90 - Medicine and Allied Occupations (Continuation)	46
Chapter 90 - Medicine and Allied Occupations (Continuation)	47
Chapter 90 - Medicine and Allied Occupations (Continuation)	48
Chapter 90A - Sanitarians and Water and Wastewater Treatment Facility Operators	48
Chapter 90B - Social Worker Certification and Licensure Act	48
Chapter 90C - North Carolina Recreational Therapy Licensure Act	48
Chapter 90D - Interpreters and Transliterators	48
Chapter 91 - Pawnbrokers [Repealed.]	48
Chapter 91A - Pawnbrokers Modernization Act of 1989	48
Chapter 92 - Photographers [Deleted.]	48
Chapter 93 - Certified Public Accountants	48
Chapter 93A - Real Estate License Law	49
Chapter 93B - Occupational Licensing Boards	49
Chapter 93C - Watchmakers [Repealed.]	49
Chapter 93D - North Carolina State Hearing Aid Dealers and Fitters Board.	49
Chapter 93E - North Carolina Appraisers Act	49
Chapter 94 - Apprenticeship	49
Chapter 95 - Department of Labor and Labor Regulations	49
Chapter 95 - Department of Labor and Labor Regulations (Continuation)	50
Chapter 96 - Employment Security	50
Chapter 97 - Workers' Compensation Act	50
Chapter 97 - Workers' Compensation Act (Continuation)	51

Chapter 98 - Burnt and Lost Records	51
Chapter 99 - Libel and Slander	51
Chapter 99A - Civil Remedies for Criminal Actions	51
Chapter 99B - Products Liability	51
Chapter 99C - Actions Relating to Winter Sports Safety and Accidents	51
Chapter 99D - Civil Rights	51
Chapter 99E - Special Liability Provisions	51
Chapter 100 - Monuments, Memorials and Parks	51
Chapter 101 - Names of Persons	51
Chapter 102 - Official Survey Base	51
Chapter 103 - Sundays, Holidays and Special Days	51
Chapter 104 - United States Lands	51
Chapter 104A - Degrees of Kinship	51
Chapter 104B - Hurricanes or Other Acts of Nature	51
Chapter 104C - Atomic Energy, Radioactivity and Ionizing Radiation [Repealed and Recodified.]	51
Chapter 104D - Southern States Energy Compact	51
Chapter 104E - North Carolina Radiation Protection Act	51
Chapter 104F - Southeast Interstate Low-Level Radioactive Waste Management Compact [Repealed]	51
Chapter 104G - North Carolina Low-Level Radioactive Waste Management Authority Act of 1987 [Repealed]	51
Chapter 105 - Taxation	51
Chapter 105 - Taxation (Continuation)	52
Chapter 105 - Taxation (Continuation)	53
Chapter 105 - Taxation (Continuation)	54
Chapter 105A - Setoff Debt Collection Act	55
Chapter 105B - Defaulted Student Loan Recovery Act	55
Chapter 106 - Agriculture	55
Chapter 106 - Agriculture (Continue)	56
Chapter 106 - Agriculture (Continue)	57
Chapter 107 - Agricultural Development Districts [Repealed.]	57
Chapter 108 - Social Services [Repealed and Recodified.]	57
Chapter 108A - Social Services	57
Chapter 108B - Community Action Programs	58
Chapter 108C Medicaid and Health Choice Provider Requirements.	58
Chapter 108D Medicaid Managed Care for Behavioral Health Services.	58
Chapter 109 - Bonds [Recodified.]	58
Chapter 110 - Child Welfare	58
Chapter 111 - Aid to the Blind	58
Chapter 112 - Confederate Homes and Pensions [Repealed.]	58
Chapter 113 - Conservation and Development	58
Chapter 113 - Conservation and Development (Continuation)	59

Chapter 113A - Pollution Control and Environment	59
Chapter 113A - Pollution Control and Environment (Continuation)	60
Chapter 113B - North Carolina Energy Policy Act of 1975	60
Chapter 114 - Department of Justice	60
Chapter 115 - Elementary and Secondary Education [Repealed.]	60
Chapter 115A - Community Colleges, Technical Institutes, and Industrial Education Centers [Repealed.]	60
Chapter 115B - Tuition and Fee Waivers	60
Chapter 115C - Elementary and Secondary Education	60
Chapter 115C - Elementary and Secondary Education (Continuation)	61
Chapter 115C - Elementary and Secondary Education (Continuation)	62
Chapter 115C - Elementary and Secondary Education (Continuation)	63
Chapter 115D - Community Colleges	63
Chapter 115E - Private Educational Facilities Finance Act [Recodified]	63
Chapter 116 - Higher Education	63
Chapter 116 - Higher Education (Continuation)	63
Chapter 116A - Escheats and Abandoned Property [Repealed.]	64
Chapter 116B - Escheats and Abandoned Property	64
Chapter 116C - Continuum of Education Programs	64
Chapter 116D - Higher Education Bonds	64
Chapter 116E -Education Longitudinal Data System	64
Chapter 117 - Electrification	64
Chapter 118 - Firemen's and Rescue Squad Workers' Relief and Pension Funds [Recodified.]	64
Chapter 118A - Firemen's Death Benefit Act [Repealed.]	64
Chapter 118B - Members of a Rescue Squad Death Benefit Act [Repealed.]	64
Chapter 119 - Gasoline and Oil Inspection and Regulation	64
Chapter 120 - General Assembly	65
Chapter 120 - General Assembly (Continuation)	66
Chapter 120 - General Assembly (Continuation)	67
Chapter 120C - Lobbying	67
Chapter 121 - Archives and History	67
Chapter 122 - Hospitals for the Mentally Disordered [Repealed.]	67
Chapter 122A - North Carolina Housing Finance Agency	67
Chapter 122B - North Carolina Agricultural Facilities Finance Act [Repealed.]	67
Chapter 122C - Mental Health, Developmental Disabilities, and Substance Abuse Act of 1985	67
Chapter 122C - Mental Health, Developmental Disabilities, and Substance Abuse Act of 1985 (Continuation)	68

Chapter 122D - North Carolina Agricultural Finance Act	68
Chapter 122E - North Carolina Housing Trust and Oil Overcharge Act	68
Chapter 123 - Impeachment	69
Chapter 123A - Industrial Development [Repealed.]	69
Chapter 124 - Internal Improvements	69
Chapter 125 - Libraries	69
Chapter 126 - State Personnel System	69
Chapter 127 - Militia [Repealed.]	69
Chapter 127A - Militia	69
Chapter 127B - Military Affairs	69
Chapter 127C - Advisory Commission on Military Affairs	69
Chapter 128 - Offices and Public Officers	69
Chapter 128 - Offices and Public Officers (Continuation)	70
Chapter 129 - Public Buildings and Grounds	70
Chapter 130 - Public Health [Repealed.]	70
Chapter 130A - Public Health	70
Chapter 130A - Public Health (Continuation)	71
Chapter 130A - Public Health (Continuation)	72
Chapter 130B - Hazardous Waste Management Commission [Repealed.]	72
Chapter 131 - Public Hospitals [Repealed.]	72
Chapter 131A - Health Care Facilities Finance Act	72
Chapter 131B - Licensing of Ambulatory Surgical Facilities [Repealed.]	72
Chapter 131C - Charitable Solicitation Licensure Act [Repealed.]	72
Chapter 131D - Inspection and Licensing of Facilities	72
Chapter 131E - Health Care Facilities and Services	72
Chapter 131E - Health Care Facilities and Services (Continuation)	73
Chapter 131F - Solicitation of Contributions	73
Chapter 132 - Public Records	73
Chapter 133 - Public Works	74
Chapter 134 - Youth Development [Recodified.]	74
Chapter 134A - Youth Services [Repealed.]	74
Chapter 135 - Retirement System for Teachers and State Employees; Social Security; Health Insurance Program for Children	74
Chapter 135 - Retirement System for Teachers and State Employees; Social Security; Health Insurance Program for Children	75
Chapter 136 - Transportation	75
Chapter 136 - Transportation (Continuation)	76
Chapter 137 - Rural Rehabilitation [Repealed.]	76
Chapter 138 - Salaries, Fees and Allowances	76
Chapter 138A - State Government Ethics Act	76

Chapter	Page
Chapter 139 - Soil and Water Conservation Districts	76
Chapter 140 - State Art Museum; Symphony and Art Societies	76
Chapter 140A - State Awards System	76
Chapter 141 - State Boundaries	76
Chapter 142 - State Debt	76
Chapter 143 - State Departments, Institutions, and Commissions	77
Chapter 143 - State Departments, Institutions, and Commissions (Continuation)	78
Chapter 143 - State Departments, Institutions, and Commissions (Continuation)	79
Chapter 143 - State Departments, Institutions, and Commissions (Continuation)	80
Chapter 143A - State Government Reorganization	80
Chapter 143B - Executive Organization Act of 1973	80
Chapter 143B - Executive Organization Act of 1973 (Continuation)	81
Chapter 143B - Executive Organization Act of 1973 (Continuation)	82
Chapter 143C - State Budget Act	83
Chapter 143D - The State Governmental Accountability and Internal Control Act	83
Chapter 144 - State Flag, Official Governmental Flags, Motto, and Colors	83
Chapter 145 - State Symbols and Other Official Adoptions.	83
Chapter 146 - State Lands	83
Chapter 147 - State Officers	83
Chapter 148 - State Prison System	84
Chapter 149 - State Song and Toast	84
Chapter 150 - Uniform Revocation of Licenses [Repealed.]	84
Chapter 150A - Administrative Procedure Act [Recodified.]	84
Chapter 150B - Administrative Procedure Act	84
Chapter 151 - Constables [Repealed.]	84
Chapter 152 - Coroners	84
Chapter 152A - County Medical Examiner [Repealed.]	84
Chapter 152A - County Medical Examiner [Repealed.] (Continuation)	85
Chapter 153 - Counties and County Commissioners [Repealed.]	85
Chapter 153A - Counties	85
Chapter 153B - Mountain Resources Planning Act	85
Chapter 153C - Uwharrie Regional Resources Act	85
Chapter 154 - County Surveyor [Repealed.]	85
Chapter 155 - County Treasurer [Repealed.]	85
Chapter 156 - Drainage	85

Chapter 156 – Drainage (Continuation)	86
Chapter 157 - Housing Authorities and Projects	86
Chapter 157A - Historic Properties Commissions [Transferred.]	86
Chapter 158 - Local Development	86
Chapter 159 - Local Government Finance	86
Chapter 159 - Local Government Finance (Continuation)	87
Chapter 159A - Pollution Abatement and Industrial Facilities Financing Act [Unconstitutional.]	87
Chapter 159B - Joint Municipal Electric Power and Energy Act	87
Chapter 159C - Industrial and Pollution Control Facilities Financing Act	87
Chapter 159D - The North Carolina Capital Facilities Financing Act	87
Chapter 159E - Registered Public Obligations Act	87
Chapter 159F - North Carolina Energy Development Authority [Repealed.]	87
Chapter 159G - Water Infrastructure	87
Chapter 159H - [Reserved.]	87
Chapter 159I - Solid Waste Management Loan Program and Local Government Special Obligation Bonds	87
Chapter 160 - Municipal Corporations [Repealed And Transferred.]	87
Chapter 160A - Cities and Towns	88
Chapter 160A - Cities and Towns (Continuation)	89
Chapter 160B - Consolidated City-County Act	89
Chapter 160C - Baseball Park Districts [Repealed.]	90
Chapter 161 - Register of Deeds	90
Chapter 162 - Sheriff	90
Chapter 162A - Water and Sewer Systems	90
Chapter 162B Continuity of Local Government in Emergency.	90
Chapter 163 Elections and Election Laws.	90
Chapter 163 Elections and Election Laws. (Continuation)	91
Chapter 164 Concerning the General Statutes of North Carolina.	92
Chapter 165 Veterans.	92
Chapter 166 Civil Preparedness Agencies [Repealed.]	92
Chapter 166A North Carolina Emergency Management Act.	92
Chapter 167 State Civil Air Patrol [Repealed.]	92
Chapter 168 Persons with Disabilities.	92
Chapter 168A Persons With Disabilities Protection Act.	92

Chapter 164.

Concerning the General Statutes of North Carolina.

Article 1.

The General Statutes.

§ 164-1. Title of revision.

This revision shall be known as the "General Statutes of North Carolina" and may be cited in either of the following ways: "General Statutes of North Carolina"; or "General Statutes"; or "G.S."; or "N.C. Gen. Stat."; or "N.C.G.S." (1985, c. 609, s. 6.)

§ 164-2. Effect as to repealing other statutes.

All public and general statutes not contained in the General Statutes of North Carolina are hereby repealed with the exceptions and limitations hereafter mentioned in this Chapter. No statute or law which has been heretofore repealed shall be revived by the repeal contained in any of the sections of the General Statutes of North Carolina or by the omission of any repealing statute from the General Statutes. All public and general statutes enacted at the regular session of the General Assembly of 1943 shall be deemed to repeal any conflicting provisions of the General Statutes of North Carolina.

§ 164-3. Repeal not to affect rights accrued or suits commenced.

The repeal of the statutes described in G.S. 164-2 shall not affect any act done, any right accruing, accrued or established, or any action or proceeding had or commenced in any case before the time when such repeal shall take effect, but the proceedings in any such case shall be conformed, when necessary, to the provisions of the General Statutes of North Carolina.

§ 164-4. Offenses, penalties and liabilities not affected.
No offense committed, no penalty or forfeiture incurred, no liability arising, and no remedy availed of, under any of the statutes hereby repealed, before the time when such repeal shall take effect shall be affected by the repeal.

§ 164-5. Pending actions and proceedings not affected.

No action or proceeding pending at the time of the repeal, for any offense committed, or for the recovery of any penalty or forfeiture incurred under any of the statutes hereby repealed shall be affected by such repeal, except that the proceedings in such action or proceeding shall be conformed, when necessary, to the provisions of the General Statutes of North Carolina.

§ 164-6. Effect of repeal on persons holding office.

All persons who at the time the General Statutes of North Carolina becomes effective shall hold any office under any of the statutes hereby repealed shall continue to hold the same according to the tenure thereof.

§ 164-7. Statutes not repealed.

The General Statutes of North Carolina shall not have the effect of repealing statutes or provisions of statutes which affect only a particular locality, public-local or private statutes, statutes exempting pending litigation from operation of statutes, statutes relating to the boundary of the State or of any county, acts ceding or relating to the ceding of lands of the State to the federal government, statutes relating to the Cherokee lands, statutes relating to the construction or interpretation of statutes, statutes by virtue of which bonds have been issued and are outstanding on the effective date of the General Statutes, validating acts or curative statutes, or acts granting pensions to named individuals if such statutes were in force on the effective date of the General Statutes.

§ 164-8. General Statutes of North Carolina effective December 31, 1943.

All provisions, chapters, subdivisions of chapters and sections contained in the General Statutes of North Carolina shall be in force from and after the thirty-first day of December 1943.

§ 164-9. Completion of General Statutes by Division of Legislative Drafting and Codification of Statutes.

The Division of Legislative Drafting and Codification of Statutes of the State Department of Justice, under the direction and supervision of the Attorney General, shall complete and perfect the General Statutes, as enacted by the General Assembly of 1943, by changing all references therein to the "Code," "North Carolina Code," "Code of 1943" or "North Carolina Code of 1943" to read "General Statutes," and by causing to be inserted therein all such general public statutes as may be enacted at the 1943 Session of the General Assembly and all amendments, in their proper places in sections under the appropriate chapter and subdivisions of chapters, and by deleting all sections or portions of sections found to be expressly repealed, or found to be repealed by virtue of the repeal of any cognate sections or parts of sections of the Consolidated Statutes or session laws, and by deleting repealed provisions and substituting in lieu thereof all proper amendments of the General Statutes or of cognate sections of the Consolidated Statutes or session laws; and the Division is hereby authorized to change the number of sections and chapters, transfer sections, chapters and subdivisions of chapters and make such other corrections which do not change the law, as may be found by the Division necessary in making an accurate, clear, and orderly statement of said laws. After the completion of such codification of the general and public laws of 1943, such laws, as they appear in the printed volumes of the General Statutes, shall be deemed an accurate codification of the statutes of 1943 contained therein. (1943, c. 15, s. 3.)

§ 164-10. Supplements to the General Statutes; rearrangement of laws, and correction of errors.

The Legislative Services Office shall have the following duties and powers with regard to the supplements to the General Statutes:

(1)   Within six months after the adjournment of each General Assembly, or as soon thereafter as possible, the Legislative Services Office shall cause to be published under its supervision, cumulative supplements to the General Statutes, and any replacement or recompiled volumes thereof, which shall contain an accurate transcription of all laws of a general and permanent nature enacted by the General Assembly, the material contained in the next preceding supplement, complete and accurate annotations to the statutes, appendix and other material accumulated since the publication of the next preceding supplement, and a cumulative index of said material.

(2)   Periodically, every six months after the publication and issuance of a cumulative supplement following a session of the General Assembly, or as soon

thereafter as possible, the Legislative Services Office shall cause to be published an interim supplement containing all pertinent annotations and other material found by the Legislative Services Office to be necessary and proper, accumulating since the publication of the said cumulative supplement or the last interim supplement.

(3) In the preparation of the general and permanent laws enacted by the General Assembly the Legislative Services Office is hereby authorized:

a. To rearrange the order of chapters, subchapters, articles, sections and other divisions or subdivisions;

b. To provide titles for any such divisions or subdivisions and section titles or catchlines when they are not provided by such laws;

c. To adopt a uniform system of lettering or numbering sections and the various subdivisions thereof and to reletter or renumber sections and section subdivisions in accordance with such uniform system;

d. To rearrange definitions in alphabetical order;

e. To rearrange lists of counties in alphabetical order; and

f. To make such other changes in arrangement and form that do not change the law as may be found by the Legislative Services Office necessary for an accurate, clear and orderly codification of such general and permanent laws. (1945, c. 863; 1947, c. 150; 1951, c. 1149, s. 1; 1957, c. 1013; 2011-97, s. 3.)

§ 164-11. Supplements prima facie statement of laws; method of citation.

(a) The supplements to the General Statutes of North Carolina, or to any replacement or recompiled volumes of the General Statutes, when printed under the supervision of the Legislative Services Office shall establish prima facie the general and permanent laws of North Carolina contained in said supplements.

(b) The cumulative pocket supplement may be cited as "G.S., Supp. 19 _____" and the interim supplement may be cited as _____ G.S. In. Supp. 19 _____," the blank in front of "G.S." to be filled in with the number of the interim supplement for that year. (1945, c. 863; 1951, c. 1149, s. 2; 2011-97, s. 4.)

§ 164-11.1. Cumulative Supplements prima facie evidence of laws.

The 1945, 1947, 1949, 1951, 1953, 1955, and 1957 Cumulative Supplements to the General Statutes of North Carolina, or to any replacement or recompiled volumes of the General Statutes as compiled and published by The Michie Company under the supervision of the Department of Justice of the State of North Carolina, are hereby constituted and declared to be prima facie evidence of the laws of North Carolina contained in said supplements. (1949, c. 45; 1951, c. 1149, s. 3; 1953, c. 140; 1955, c. 53; 1957, c. 371.)

§ 164-11.2. Adoption of 1950 Volumes 2A, 2B and 2C of the General Statutes.

The chapters, subchapters, articles and sections, now comprising Volume 2 of the General Statutes of North Carolina and the Cumulative Supplements thereto, consisting of G.S. 26-1 through 105-462 now in force as amended, are hereby reenacted and designated Volumes 2A, 2B and 2C, respectively, of the General Statutes of North Carolina: Provided, that this enactment of Volumes 2A, 2B and 2C shall not include any appended annotations, editorial notes, comments, cross references, legislative or historical references, or other material collateral or supplemental to the said chapters, subchapters, articles and sections, but not contained in the body thereof. (1951, c. 900.)

§ 164-11.3. Adoption of 1952 Volumes 3A, 3B and 3C of the General Statutes.

The chapters, subchapters, articles and sections now comprising Volume 3 of the General Statutes of North Carolina, and Cumulative Supplements thereto, consisting of G.S. 106-1 through 166-13, now in force, as amended, are hereby reenacted and designated Volumes 3A, 3B and 3C respectively of the General Statutes of North Carolina. This reenactment of Volumes 3A, 3B and 3C shall not be construed to invalidate or repeal any acts which have been passed during the 1953 Session of the General Assembly, prior to February 18, 1953, nor shall this reenactment include any appended annotations, editorial notes, comments and cross references, legislative or historical references, or other material connected or supplemental to the said chapters, subchapters, articles and sections, but not contained in the body hereof. (1955, c. 43.)

§ 164-11.4. Adoption of 1953 Volumes 1A, 1B and 1C of the General Statutes.

The chapters, subchapters, articles and sections now comprising Volume 1 of the General Statutes of North Carolina, and Cumulative Supplements thereto, consisting of G.S. 1-1 through 27-59, now in force, as amended, are hereby reenacted and designated Volumes 1A, 1B and 1C respectively of the General Statutes of North Carolina. This enactment of Volumes 1A, 1B and 1C shall not be construed to invalidate or repeal any acts which have been passed during the 1955 Session of the General Assembly, prior to February 11, 1955, nor shall this enactment include any appended annotations, editorial notes, comments and cross references, legislative or historical references, or other material connected or supplemental to the said chapters, subchapters, articles and sections, but not contained in the body hereof. (1955, c. 43.)

§ 164-11.5. Adoption of 1958 Replacement Volumes 2C and 3B of the General Statutes.

(a) The chapters, subchapters, articles and sections now comprising Volume 2C of the General Statutes of North Carolina, and Cumulative Supplement thereto, consisting of G.S. 83-1 through 105-462, now in force, as amended, are hereby reenacted and designated Replacement Volume 2C of the General Statutes of North Carolina.

(b) The chapters, subchapters, articles and sections now comprising Volume 3B of the General Statutes of North Carolina, and Cumulative Supplement thereto, consisting of G.S. 117-1 through 150-34, now in force, as amended, are hereby reenacted and designated Replacement Volume 3B of the General Statutes of North Carolina.

(c) This enactment of Replacement Volumes 2C and 3B shall not be construed to invalidate or repeal any acts which have been passed during the 1959 Session of the General Assembly, prior to February 24, 1959, nor shall this enactment include any appended annotations, editorial notes, comments and cross references, legislative or historical references, or other material connected or supplemental to the said chapters, subchapters, articles and sections, but not contained in the body hereof. (1959, c. 12.)

§ 164-11.6. Adoption of 1960 Replacement Volumes 2B and 3A of the General Statutes.

(a) The chapters, subchapters, articles and sections now comprising Volume 2B of the General Statutes of North Carolina, and Cumulative Supplement thereto, consisting of G.S. 53-1 through 82-18, now in force, as amended, are hereby reenacted and designated as Replacement Volume 2B of the General Statutes of North Carolina.

(b) The chapters, subchapters, articles and sections now comprising Volume 3A of the General Statutes of North Carolina, and Cumulative Supplement thereto, consisting of G.S. 106-1 through 116-185, now in force, as amended, are hereby reenacted and designated Replacement Volume 3A of the General Statutes of North Carolina.

(c) This enactment of Replacement Volumes 2B and 3A shall not be construed to invalidate or repeal any acts which have been passed during the 1961 Session of the General Assembly, prior to March 14, 1961, nor shall this enactment include any appended annotations, editorial notes, comments and cross references, legislative or historical references, or other material connected or supplemental to the said chapters, subchapters, articles and sections, but not contained in the body hereof. (1961, cc. 38, 185; 2012-156, s. 49; 2012-194, s 53.)

§ 164-11.7. Adoption of 1965 Replacement Volumes 2B, 2C and 2D and 1964 Replacement Volumes 3B, 3C and 3D of the General Statutes.

(a) The chapters, subchapters, articles and sections now comprising Volumes 2B and 2C of the General Statutes of North Carolina, and Cumulative Supplements thereto, consisting of G.S. 53-1 to 105-462, now in force, as amended, are hereby reenacted and designated as 1965 Replacement Volumes 2B, 2C and 2D of the General Statutes of North Carolina.

(b) The chapters, subchapters, articles and sections now comprising Volumes 3B and 3C of the General Statutes of North Carolina, and Cumulative Supplements thereto, consisting of G.S. 117-1 to 167-3, now in force, as amended, are hereby reenacted and designated as 1964 Replacement Volumes 3B, 3C and 3D of the General Statutes of North Carolina.

(c) This enactment of 1965 Replacement Volumes 2B, 2C and 2D and 1964 Replacement Volumes 3B, 3C and 3D shall not be construed to invalidate or repeal any acts which have been passed during the 1965 Session of the General Assembly, prior to May 14, 1965, nor shall this enactment include any appended annotations, editorial notes, comments and cross references, legislative or historical references, or other material connected or supplemental to the said chapters, subchapters, articles and sections, but not contained in the body hereof. (1965, c. 544; 2012-156, s. 50; 2012-194, s 53.)

§ 164-11.8. Adoption of 1965 Replacement Volumes 1C and 1D and 1966 Replacement Volumes 2A and 3A of the General Statutes.

(a)   The chapters, subchapters, articles and sections now comprising Volume 1C of the General Statutes of North Carolina, and Cumulative Supplements thereto, consisting of G.S. 15-1 to 27-59, now in force, as amended, are hereby reenacted and designated as 1965 Replacement Volumes 1C and 1D of the General Statutes of North Carolina.

(b)   The chapters, subchapters, articles and sections now comprising 1950 Recompiled Volume 2A of the General Statutes of North Carolina, and Cumulative Supplements thereto, consisting of G.S. 28-1 to 52A-20, now in force, as amended, is hereby reenacted and designated as 1966 Replacement Volume 2A of the General Statutes of North Carolina.

(c)   The chapters, subchapters, articles and sections now comprising 1960 Replacement Volume 3A of the General Statutes of North Carolina, and Cumulative Supplements thereto, consisting of G.S. 106-1 to 116-211, now in force, as amended, is hereby reenacted and designated as 1066 Replacement Volume 3A of the General Statutes of North Carolina.

(d)   This enactment of 1965 Replacement Volumes 1C and 1D and 1966 Replacement Volumes 2A and 3A shall not be construed to invalidate or repeal any acts which have been passed during the 1967 Session of the General Assembly, prior to the date of ratification, nor shall this enactment include any appended annotations, editorial notes, comments and cross references, legislative or historical references, or other material connected or supplemental to said chapters, subchapters, articles and sections, but not contained in the body hereof. (1967, c. 1266.)

§ 164-11.9. Adoption of 1969 Replacement Volumes 1A and 1B of the General Statutes.

(a) The chapters and sections thereof now comprising Volume 1A of the General Statutes of North Carolina, and Cumulative Supplement thereto, consisting of G.S. 1-1 through 1B-8 now in force, as amended, are hereby reenacted and designated as 1969 Replacement Volume 1A of the General Statutes of North Carolina.

(b) The chapters and sections thereof now comprising Volume 1B of the General Statutes of North Carolina and Cumulative Supplement thereto, consisting of G.S. 2-1 through 14-431, now in force, as amended, are hereby reenacted and designated as 1969 Replacement Volume 1B of the General Statutes of North Carolina.

This reenactment and designation shall not operate as ratification of the judgment of the editors in placing certain sections of this volume in the "1970 Interim Supplement" to Volume 1B. Such sections shall be treated in all respects as if they appear within the bound replacement volume. (1971, c. 135.)

Article 2.

The General Statutes Commission.

§ 164-12. Creation; name.

(a) There is hereby created and established a commission to be known as "The General Statutes Commission."

(b) The Commission shall be located within the General Assembly for administrative purposes only. (1945, c. 157; 2011-97, s. 5.)

§ 164-13. Duties; use of funds.

(a) It shall be the duty of the Commission:

(1) To advise and cooperate with the Legislative Services Office in the work of continuous statute research and correction for which the Legislative Services Office is made responsible by G.S. 120-36.21(2).

(2) To advise and cooperate with the Legislative Services Office in the preparation and issuance of supplements to the General Statutes pursuant to G.S. 120-36.21(1).

(3) To make a continuing study of all matters involved in the preparation and publication of modern codes of law.

(4) To recommend to the General Assembly the enactment of such substantive changes in the law as the Commission may deem advisable.

(5) To receive and consider proposed changes in the law recommended by the American Law Institute, by the National Conference of Commissioners on Uniform State Laws or by other learned bodies.

(b) Funds made available to the Commission by appropriation of the General Assembly, by allotment from the Contingency and Emergency Fund, or otherwise, may be used to employ the services of persons especially qualified to assist in the work of the Commission and for necessary clerical assistance. (1945, c. 157; 1951, c. 761; 1957, c. 1405; 1969, c. 541, s. 3; 1971, c. 1093, s. 7; 1981, c. 599, s. 20; 2011-97, s. 6.)

§ 164-14. Membership; appointments; terms; vacancies.

(a) The Commission shall consist of 14 members, who shall be appointed as follows:

(1) One member, by the president of the North Carolina State Bar;

(2) One member, by the General Statutes Commission;

(3) One member, by the dean of the school of law of the University of North Carolina;

(4) One member, by the dean of the school of law of Duke University;

(5) One member, by the dean of the school of law of Wake Forest University;

(6) One member, by the Speaker of the House of Representatives of each General Assembly from the membership of the House;

(7)   One member, by the President Pro Tempore of the Senate of each General Assembly from the membership of the Senate;

(8)   Two members, by the Governor;

(9)   One member, by the dean of the school of law of North Carolina Central University;

(10)   One member by the president of the North Carolina Bar Association;

(11)   One member, by the dean of the school of law of Campbell University.

(12)   One member, by the dean of the school of law of Elon University.

(13)   One member, by the dean of the Charlotte School of Law (NC), Inc.

(b)   Appointments of original members of the Commission made by the president of the North Carolina State Bar, the president of the North Carolina Bar Association, and the deans of the schools of law of Duke University, the University of North Carolina, and Wake Forest University shall be for one year. Appointments of original members of the Commission made by the Speaker of the House of Representatives, the President of the Senate, and the Governor shall be for two years.

(c)   After the appointment of the original members of the Commission, appointments by the president of the North Carolina State Bar, the General Statutes Commission, and the deans of the schools of law of North Carolina Central University, Duke University, Elon University, the University of North Carolina, and Wake Forest University shall be made in the even-numbered years, and appointments made by the Speaker of the House of Representatives, the President Pro Tempore of the Senate, president of the North Carolina Bar Association, the deans of the School of Law of Campbell University and the Charlotte School of Law (NC), Inc., and the Governor shall be made in the odd-numbered years. Such appointments shall be made for two-year terms beginning June first of the year when such appointments are to become effective and expiring May 31 two years thereafter. All such appointments shall be made not later than May 31 of the year when such appointments are to become effective.

(d)   If any appointment provided for by this section is not made prior to June first of the year when it should become effective, a vacancy shall exist with respect thereto, and the vacancy shall then be filled by appointment by the Governor. If any member of the Commission dies or resigns during the term for which he was appointed, his successor for the unexpired term shall be appointed by the person who made the original appointment, as provided in G.S. 164-14, or by the successor of such person; and if such vacancy is not filled within 30 days after the vacancy occurs, it shall then be filled by appointment by the Governor. In any case where an appointment authorized to be made by G.S. 164-14(c) has not been made on or before July 31 of the year in which it was due to be made, a vacancy shall exist with respect to that appointment and the General Statutes Commission at its next meeting shall by majority vote fill the vacancy by appointment.

(e)   All appointments shall be reported to the secretary of the Commission.

(f)   Notwithstanding the expiration of the term of the appointment, the terms of members of the General Statutes Commission shall continue until the appointment of a successor has been made and reported to the secretary of the Commission. (1945, cc. 157, 635; 1947, c. 114, s. 3; 1967, cc. 17, 1230; 1969, c. 541, s. 4; 1971, c. 1, ss. 1, 2; c. 76; 1975, c. 394, ss. 1, 2; 1977, c. 709, ss. 1, 2; 1991, c. 739, s. 33; 1995, c. 509, s. 119; 2009-550, s. 8(a).)

§ 164-15. Meetings; quorum.

The Commission shall hold not less than two regular meetings each year, of which one shall be held in June and one in November, at such times during those months as may be fixed therefor by the Commission itself. The Commission may establish a schedule for other regular meetings. Special meetings may be called by the chairman, or by any two members of the Commission, upon such notice and in such manner as may be fixed therefor by the policies adopted by the Commission. The regular June and November meetings of the Commission shall be held in Raleigh, but the Commission may provide for the holding of other meetings from time to time at any other place or places in the State. A majority of the members of the Commission shall constitute a quorum. (1945, c. 157; 1983, c. 768, s. 24; 2011-97, s. 7.)

§ 164-16. Officers.

At its regular June meeting in the odd-numbered years the Commission shall elect a chairman and a vice-chairman for a term of two years and until their successors are elected and assume the duties of their positions. The Revisor of Statutes shall be ex officio secretary of the Commission. (1945, c. 157; 1947, c. 114, s. 2.)

§ 164-17. Committees.

The Commission may elect, or may authorize its chairman to appoint, such committees of the Commission as it may deem proper. The Commission may adopt such policies and guidelines not inconsistent with this Article as it may deem proper with respect to any and all matters relating to the discharge of its duties under this Article. (1945, c. 157; 2011-97, s. 8.)

§ 164-18. Reports.

The Commission shall submit to each regular session of the General Assembly a report of its work during the preceding two years, together with such recommendations as it may deem proper. The Commission may report recommended legislation to each annual session of the General Assembly as it deems appropriate. (1945, c. 157; 2011-97, s. 9.)

§ 164-19. Compensation.

Members of the Commission shall be paid the amount of per diem provided by G.S. 138-5 for attendance upon meetings of the Commission, or upon attendance of meetings of committees of the Commission, together with such subsistence and travel allowance as may be provided by law. (1945, c. 157; 1969, c. 445, s. 3.)

§§ 164-20 through 164-24. Reserved for future codification purposes.

Article 3.

Commission on Code Recodification.

§§ 164-25 through 164-34: Repealed by Session Laws 1981, c. 859, s. 13.10.

Article 4.

Sentencing Commission.

§ 164-35. Commission established.

The North Carolina Sentencing and Policy Advisory Commission is established. As used in this Article, the term "Commission" means the North Carolina Sentencing and Policy Advisory Commission. (1989 (Reg. Sess., 1990), c. 1076, s. 1; 1991 (Reg. Sess., 1992), c. 812, s. 12; c. 816, s. 1; 1993, c. 253, s. 5.1; c. 321, s. 200.1; 1993 (Reg. Sess., 1994), c. 591, s. 6(a); 1995, c. 236, s. 1; 1997-256, s. 6; 1997-347, s. 2; 1997-401, s. 2; 1997-418, s. 2; 1997-443, s. 18.6(a).)

§ 164-36. Powers and duties.

(a) Sentences established for violations of the State's criminal laws should be based on the established purposes of our criminal justice and corrections systems. The Commission shall evaluate sentencing laws and policies in relationship to both the stated purposes of the criminal justice and corrections systems and the availability of sentencing options. The Commission shall make recommendations to the General Assembly for the modification of sentencing laws and policies, and for the addition, deletion, or expansion of sentencing options as necessary to achieve policy goals. The Commission shall make a report of its recommendations, including any recommended legislation, to the General Assembly annually.

(b) Dispositions established for violations by juveniles of the State's criminal laws should be based on the established purposes set forth in Chapter 7B of the General Statutes. The Commission shall evaluate dispositional laws and policies in relationship to both the stated purposes of Chapter 7B of the General Statutes and the availability of dispositional alternatives. The Commission shall make recommendations to the General Assembly for the modification of dispositional laws and policies, and for the addition, deletion, or expansion of dispositional alternatives as necessary to achieve policy goals. The Commission shall make a report of its recommendations, including any recommended legislation, to the General Assembly annually. (1989 (Reg. Sess., 1990), c. 1076, s. 1; 1991 (Reg. Sess., 1992), c. 812, s. 12; c. 816, s. 1; 1993, c. 253, s. 5.1; c. 321, s. 200.1; 1993 (Reg. Sess., 1994), c. 591, s. 6(a); 1995, c. 236, s. 1;

1997-256, s. 6; 1997-347, s. 2; 1997-401, s. 2; 1997-418, s. 2; 1997-443, s. 18.6(a); 1997-443, s. 18.6(c); 1998-202, s. 10(a).)

§ 164-37. Membership; chairman; meetings; quorum.

The Commission shall consist of 28 members as follows:

(1)   The Chief Justice of the North Carolina Supreme Court shall appoint a sitting or former Justice or judge of the General Court of Justice, who shall serve as Chairman of the Commission;

(2)   The Chief Judge of the North Carolina Court of Appeals, or another judge on the Court of Appeals, serving as his designee;

(3)   The Secretary of Public Safety or his designee;

(4)   Repealed by Session Laws 2011-391, s. 43(e), effective January 1, 2011.

(5)   The Chairman of the Parole Commission, or his designee;

(6)   The President of the Conference of Superior Court Judges or his designee;

(7)   The President of the District Court Judges Association or his designee;

(8)   The President of the North Carolina Sheriff's Association or his designee;

(9)   The President of the North Carolina Association of Chiefs of Police or his designee;

(10)   One member of the public at large, who is not currently licensed to practice law in North Carolina, to be appointed by the Governor;

(11)   One member to be appointed by the Lieutenant Governor;

(12)   Three members of the House of Representatives, to be appointed by the Speaker of the House;

(13) Three members of the Senate, to be appointed by the President Pro Tempore of the Senate;

(14) The President Pro Tempore of the Senate shall appoint the representative of the North Carolina Community Sentencing Association that is recommended by the President of that organization;

(15) The Speaker of the House of Representatives shall appoint the member of the business community that is recommended by the President of the North Carolina Retail Merchants Association;

(16) The Chief Justice of the North Carolina Supreme Court shall appoint the criminal defense attorney that is recommended by the President of the North Carolina Academy of Trial Lawyers;

(17) The President of the Conference of District Attorneys or his designee;

(18) The Lieutenant Governor shall appoint the member of the North Carolina Victim Assistance Network that is recommended by the President of that organization;

(19) A rehabilitated former prison inmate, to be appointed by the Chairman of the Commission;

(20) The President of the North Carolina Association of County Commissioners or his designee;

(21) The Governor shall appoint the member of the academic community, with a background in criminal justice or corrections policy, that is recommended by the President of The University of North Carolina;

(22) The Attorney General, or a member of his staff, to be appointed by the Attorney General;

(23) The Governor shall appoint the member of the North Carolina Bar Association that is recommended by the President of that organization.

(24) A member of the Justice Fellowship Task Force, who is a resident of North Carolina, to be appointed by the Chairman of the Commission.

(25) The President of the Association of Clerks of Superior Court of North Carolina, or his designee.

(26) Repealed by Session Laws 2011-391, s. 43(e), effective January 1, 2011.

The Commission shall have its initial meeting no later than September 1, 1990, at the call of the Chairman. The Commission shall meet a minimum of four regular meetings each year. The Commission may also hold special meetings at the call of the Chairman, or by any four members of the Commission, upon such notice and in such manner as may be fixed by the rules of the Commission. A majority of the members of the Commission shall constitute a quorum. (1989 (Reg. Sess., 1990), c. 1076, s. 1; 1991 (Reg. Sess., 1992), c. 812, s. 12; c. 816, ss. 1, 2; 1993, c. 253, s. 5.1; c. 321, s. 200.1; c. 535, s. 4; 1993 (Reg. Sess., 1994), c. 591, s. 6(a); 1995, c. 236, s. 1; 1997-256, s. 6; 1997-347, s. 2; 1997-401, s. 2; 1997-418 s. 2; 1997-443, s. 18.6(a); 1998-170, s. 1; 1998-202, s. 10(f); 2000-137, s. 4(kk); 2011-145, s. 19.1(g), (i), (l); 2011-391, s. 43(c)-(e).)

§ 164-38. Terms of members; compensation; expenses.

The terms of existing members shall expire on June 30, 1997, unless they resign or are removed. New members shall be appointed or the existing members reappointed by the appointing authorities to serve terms of two years, unless they resign or are removed. Members serving by virtue of elective or appointive office or as designees of such officeholders may serve only so long as the officeholders hold those respective offices. Members appointed by the Speaker of the House and the President Pro Tempore of the Senate may be removed by the appointing authority without cause. Vacancies occurring before the expiration of a term shall be filled in the manner provided for the members first appointed. A member of the Commission may be removed only for disability, neglect of duty, incompetence, or malfeasance in office. Before removal, the member is entitled to a hearing. Effective with respect to members designated on or after July 1, 1992, a person making a designation pursuant to G.S. 164-37 may not make another designation, except that the person's successor in elective or appointive office may make a new designation.

The Commission members shall receive no salary for serving. All Commission members shall receive necessary subsistence and travel expenses in accordance with the provisions of G.S. 120-3.1, 138-5, and 138-6 as applicable. (1989 (Reg. Sess., 1990), c. 1076, s. 1; 1991 (Reg. Sess., 1992), c. 812, s. 12;

c. 816, ss. 1, 3; 1993, c. 253, s. 5.1; c. 321, s. 200.1(b); 1993 (Reg. Sess., 1994), c. 591, ss. 6(a), (b); 1995, c. 236, s. 1; c. 236, s. 2; 1997-256, s. 6; 1997-347, s. 2; 1997-401, s. 2; 1997-418, s. 2; 1997-443, s. 18.6(a); 1997-443, s. 18.6(b).)

§ 164-39. Executive director and other staff.

The Commission shall employ an Executive Director from candidates presented to it by the Chairman and the Director of the Administrative Office of the Courts. The Executive Director shall have appropriate training and experience to assist the Commission in the performance of its duties. The Executive Director shall be responsible for compiling the work of the Commission and drafting suggested legislation incorporating the Commission's findings for submission to the General Assembly.

Subject to the approval of the Chairman, the Executive Director shall employ such other staff and shall contract for services as is necessary to assist the Commission in the performance of its duties, and as funds permit.

The Commission may, with the approval of the Legislative Services Commission, meet in the State Legislative Building or the Legislative Office Building, or may meet in an area provided by the Director of the Administrative Office of the Courts. Commission staff shall use office space provided by the Director of the Administrative Office of the Courts. (1989 (Reg. Sess., 1990), c. 1076, s. 1; 1991 (Reg. Sess., 1992), c. 812, s. 12; c. 816, s. 1; 1993, c. 253, s. 5.1; c. 321, s. 200.1; 1993 (Reg. Sess., 1994), c. 591, s. 6(a); 1995, c. 236, s. 1; 1997-256, s. 6; 1997-347, s. 2; 1997-401, s. 2; 1997-418, s. 2; 1997-443, s. 18.6(a).)

§ 164-40. Correction population simulation model; Division of Juvenile Justice of the Department of Public Safety facilities population simulation model.

(a) The Commission shall develop a correctional population simulation model, and shall have first priority to apply the model to a given fact situation, or theoretical change in the sentencing laws, when requested to do so by the Chairman, the Executive Director, or the Commission as a whole.

The Executive Director or the Chairman shall make the model available to respond to inquiries by any State legislator, or by the Secretary of Public Safety, in second priority to the work of the Commission.

(b) The Commission shall develop a Division of Juvenile Justice of the Department of Public Safety facilities population simulation model, and shall have first priority to apply the model to a given fact situation, or theoretical change in the dispositional laws set forth in Chapter 7B of the General Statutes, when requested to do so by the Chairman, the Executive Director, or the Commission as a whole.

The Executive Director or the Chairman shall make the model available to respond to inquiries by any State legislator, or by the Division of Juvenile Justice of the Department of Public Safety, in second priority to the work of the Commission. (1989 (Reg. Sess., 1990), c. 1076, s. 1; 1991 (Reg. Sess., 1992), c. 812, s. 12; c. 816, s. 1; 1993, c. 253, s. 5.1; c. 321, s. 200.1; 1993 (Reg. Sess., 1994), c. 591, s. 6(a); 1995, c. 236, s. 1; 1997-256, s. 6; 1997-347, s. 2; 1997-401, s. 2; 1997-418, s. 2; 1997-443, s. 18.6(a); 1998-202, s. 10(b); 2000-137, s. 4(ii); 2011-145, s. 19.1(h), (i), (l); 2011-391, s. 43(f).)

§ 164-41. Classification of offenses - ranges of punishment.

(a) The Commission shall classify criminal offenses into felony and misdemeanor categories on the basis of their severity.

(b) In determining the proper category for each felony and misdemeanor, the Commission shall consider, to the extent that they have relevance, the following:

(1) The nature and degree of harm likely to be caused by the offense, including whether it involves property, irreplaceable property, a person, number of persons, or a breach of the public trust;

(2) The deterrent effect a particular classification may have on the commission of the offense by others;

(3) The current incidence of the offense in the State as a whole;

(4) The rights of the victim.

(c) For each classification of felonies and misdemeanors formulated pursuant to subsection (b), the Commission shall assign a suggested range of punishment. The Commission shall take into consideration the current range of punishment for each offense. (1989 (Reg. Sess., 1990), c. 1076, s. 1; 1991 (Reg. Sess., 1992), c. 812, s. 12; c. 816, s. 1; 1993, c. 253, s. 5.1; c. 321, s. 200.1; 1993 (Reg. Sess., 1994), c. 591, s. 6(a); 1995, c. 236, s. 1; 1997-256, s. 6; 1997-347, s. 2; 1997-401, s. 2; 1997-418, s. 2; 1997-443, s. 18.6(a).)

§ 164-42. Sentencing structures.

(a) The Commission shall recommend structures for use by a sentencing court in determining the most appropriate sentence to be imposed in a criminal case, including:

(1) Imposition of an active term of imprisonment;

(2) Imposition of a term of probation;

(3) Suspension of a sentence to imprisonment and imposition of probation with conditions, including the appropriate probation option or options, including house arrest, regular probation, intensive supervision, restitution, and community service;

(4) Based upon the combination of offense and defendant characteristics in each case, the presumptively appropriate length of a term of probation, or a term of imprisonment;

(5) Ordering multiple sentences to terms of imprisonment to run concurrently or consecutively;

(6) For a sentence to probation without a suspended sentence to imprisonment, the maximum term of confinement to be imposed if the defendant violates the conditions of probation.

(b) The sentencing structures shall be consistent with the goals, policies, and purposes of the criminal justice and corrections systems, as set forth in Sections 2 and 3 of the Sentencing and Policy Advisory Commission Act of 1990. As part of its work, the Commission shall offer recommendations for the incorporation of those sections into the sentencing laws of North Carolina. In formulating structures, the Commission also shall consider:

(1) The nature and characteristics of the offense;

(2) The severity of the offense in relation to other offenses;

(3) The characteristics of the defendant that mitigate or aggravate the seriousness of his criminal conduct and the punishment deserved therefor;

(4) The defendant's number of prior convictions;

(5) The available resources and constitutional capacity of the Division of Adult Correction, local confinement facilities, and community-based sanctions;

(6) The rights of the victims;

(7) That felony offenders sentenced to an active term of imprisonment, or whose suspended sentence to imprisonment is activated, should serve a designated minimum percentage of their sentences before they are eligible for parole; and

(8) That misdemeanor offenders sentenced to an active term of imprisonment, or whose suspended sentence to imprisonment is activated, should serve a designated minimum percentage of their sentence before they are eligible for parole.

(c) The Commission shall also consider the policy issues set forth in G.S. 164-42.1 in developing its sentencing structures.

(d) The Commission shall include with each set of sentencing structures a statement of its estimate of the effect of the sentencing structures on the Division of Adult Correction and local facilities, both in terms of fiscal impact and on inmate population. If the Commission finds that the proposed sentencing structures will result in inmate populations in the Division of Adult Correction and local confinement facilities that exceed the standard operating capacity, then the Commission shall present an additional set of structures that are consistent with that capacity. For purposes of this subsection, "standard operating capacity" means the total capacity expected to be available in both local confinement facilities and in the Division of Adult Correction once all the proceeds of bonds authorized by Chapter 933 of the 1989 Session Laws and Chapter 935 of the 1989 Session Laws have been expended for the construction of prison facilities. (1989 (Reg. Sess., 1990), c. 1076, s. 1; 1991 (Reg. Sess., 1992), c. 812, s. 12; c. 816, ss. 1, 5; 1993, c. 253, s. 5.1; c. 321, s. 200.1; 1993 (Reg. Sess., 1994),

c. 591, s. 6(a); 1995, c. 236, s. 1; 1997-256, s. 6; 1997-347, s. 2; 1997-401, s. 2; 1997-418, s. 2; 1997-443, s. 18.6(a); 2009-372, s. 8; 2011-145, s. 19.1(h); 2011-391, s. 43(f).)

§ 164-42.1. Policy recommendations.

(a) Using the studies of the Special Committee on Prisons, the Governor's Crime Commission, and other analyses, including testimony from representatives of the bodies that conducted the analyses, the Commission shall:

(1) Determine the long-range needs of the criminal justice and corrections systems and recommend policy priorities for those systems;

(2) Determine the long-range information needs of the criminal justice and corrections systems and acquire that information as it becomes available;

(3) Identify critical problems in the criminal justice and corrections systems and recommend strategies to solve those problems;

(4) Assess the cost-effectiveness of the use of State and local funds in the criminal justice and corrections systems;

(5) Recommend the goals, priorities, and standards for the allocation of criminal justice and corrections funds;

(6) Recommend means to improve the deterrent and rehabilitative capabilities of the criminal justice and corrections systems;

(7) Propose plans, programs, and legislation for improving the effectiveness of the criminal justice and corrections systems;

(8) Determine the sentencing structures for parole decisions;

(9) Examine the impact of mandatory sentence lengths as opposed to the deterrent effect of minimum mandatory terms of imprisonment;

(10) Examine good time and gain time practices;

(11) Study the value of presentence reports;

(12) Consider the rehabilitative potential of the offender and the appropriate rehabilitative placement;

(13) Examine the impact of imprisonment on families of offenders;

(14) Examine the impact of imprisonment on the ability of the offender to make restitution;

(15) Study the need for an amendment to Article XI, Section 1 of the State Constitution to include restitution, restraints on liberty, work programs, or other punishments to the list of punishments allowed under that section; and

(16) Study the costs and consequences of criminal behavior in North Carolina and consider the value of preventing crimes by using incarceration to deter both prospective criminals and convicted criminals from future crimes.

(b) Using the studies and analyses available, including testimony from representatives of the bodies that conducted the analyses, the Commission shall:

(1) Determine the long-range needs of the juvenile justice system and recommend policy priorities for that system;

(2) Determine the long-range information needs of the juvenile justice system and acquire that information as it becomes available;

(3) Identify critical problems in the juvenile justice system and recommend strategies to solve those problems;

(4) Assess the cost-effectiveness of the use of State and local funds in the juvenile justice system; and

(5) Recommend the goals, priorities, and standards for the allocation of juvenile justice funds. (1989 (Reg. Sess., 1990), c. 1076, s. 1; 1993, c. 253, s. 5.1; c. 321, s. 200.1; 1993 (Reg. Sess., 1994), c. 591, s. 6(a); 1995, c. 236, s. 1; 1997-256, s. 6; 1997-347, s. 2; 1997-401, s. 2; 1997-418, s. 2; 1997-443, s. 18.6(a); 1998-202, s. 10(c).)

§ 164-42.2. Community corrections.

The Commission shall recommend a comprehensive community corrections strategy and organizational structure for the State based upon the following:

(1)   A review of existing community-based corrections programs in the State;

(2)   The identification of additional types of community corrections programs, including residential programs, necessary to create an effective continuum of corrections sanctions in North Carolina;

(3)   The identification of categories of offenders who would be eligible for sentencing to community corrections programs and the impact that the use of a comprehensive range of community-based sanctions would have on sentencing practices;

(4)   A form of State oversight and coordination to ensure that community corrections programs are coordinated in order to achieve maximum impact; and

(5)   A mechanism for State funding and local community participation in the operation and implementation of community corrections programs;

(6)   An analysis of the rate of recidivism of clients under the supervision of the existing community-based corrections programs in the State, recidivism here measured as the clients committing new crimes at any time subsequent to their entry into a community-based corrections program. (1989 (Reg. Sess., 1990), c. 1076, s. 1; 1993, c. 253, s. 5.1; c. 321, s. 200.1; 1993 (Reg. Sess., 1994), c. 591, s. 6(a); 1995, c. 236, s.1; 1997-256, s. 6; 1997-347, s. 2; 1997-401, s. 2; 1997-418, s. 2; 1997-443, s. 18.6(a).)

§ 164-43. Priority of duties; reports; continuing duties.

(a)   The Commission shall have two primary duties, and other secondary duties essential to accomplishing the primary ones. The Commission may establish subcommittees or advisory committees composed of Commission members to accomplish duties imposed by this Article.

It is the legislative intent that the Commission attach priority to accomplish the following primary duties:

(1)   The classification of criminal offenses as described in G.S. 164-41 and the formulation of sentencing structures as described in G.S. 164-42; and

(2)   The formulation of proposals and recommendations as described in G.S. 164-42.1 and G.S. 164-42.2.

(b)   The Commission shall report its findings and recommendations to the 1991 General Assembly, 1991 Regular Session. The report shall describe the status of the Commission's work, and shall include any completed policy recommendations.

(c)   The Commission shall report on its progress in formulating recommendations for the classification and ranges of punishment for felonies and misdemeanors, required by G.S. 164-41, and sentencing structures, established under G.S. 164-42, to the 1991 General Assembly, 1992 Regular Session, and shall make a final report on these recommendations no later than 30 days after the convening of the 1993 Session of the General Assembly.

(d)   Once the primary duties of the Commission have been accomplished, it shall have the continuing duty to monitor and review the criminal justice and corrections systems and the juvenile justice system in this State to ensure that sentences and dispositions remain uniform and consistent, and that the goals and policies established by the State are being implemented by sentencing and dispositional practices, and it shall recommend methods by which this ongoing work may be accomplished and by which the correctional population simulation model and the Division of Juvenile Justice of the Department of Public Safety facilities population simulation model developed under G.S. 164-40 shall continue to be used by the State.

(e)   Upon adoption of a system for the classification of offenses formulated under G.S. 164-41, the Commission or its successor shall review all proposed legislation which creates a new criminal offense, changes the classification of an offense, or changes the range of punishment or dispositional level for a particular classification, and shall make recommendations to the General Assembly.

(f)   In the case of a new criminal offense, the Commission or its successor shall determine whether the proposal places the offense in the correct classification, based upon the considerations and principles set out in G.S. 164-41. If the proposal does not assign the offense to a classification, it shall be the duty of the Commission or its successor to recommend the proper classification placement.

(g) In the case of proposed changes in the classification of an offense or changes in the range of punishment or dispositional level for a classification, the Commission or its successor shall determine whether such a proposed change is consistent with the considerations and principles set out in G.S. 164-41, and shall report its findings to the General Assembly.

(h) The Commission or its successor shall meet within 10 days after the last day for filing general bills in the General Assembly for the purpose of reviewing bills as described in subsections (e), (f), and (g). The Commission or its successor shall include in its report on a bill an analysis based on an application of the correctional population simulation model or the Division of Juvenile Justice of the Department of Public Safety facilities population simulation model to the provisions of the bill. (1989 (Reg. Sess., 1990), c. 1076, s. 1; 1991 (Reg. Sess., 1992), c. 812, s. 12; c. 816, ss. 1, 4; 1993, c. 253, s. 5.1; c. 321, s. 200.1; 1993 (Reg. Sess., 1994), c. 591, s. 6(a); 1995, c. 236, s. 1; 1997-256, s. 6; 1997-347, s. 2; 1997-401, s. 2; 1997-418, s. 2; 1997-443, s. 18.6(a); 1998-202, s. 10(d); 2000-137, s. 4(jj); 2011-145, s. 19.1(l).)

§ 164-44. Statistical information; financial or other aid.

(a) The Commission shall have the secondary duty of collecting, developing, and maintaining statistical data relating to sentencing, corrections, and juvenile justice so that the primary duties of the Commission will be formulated using data that is valid, accurate, and relevant to this State. All State agencies shall provide data as it is requested by the Commission. For the purposes of G.S. 114-19.1, the Commission shall be considered to be engaged in the administration of criminal justice. All meetings of the Commission shall be open to the public and the information presented to the Commission shall be available to any State agency or member of the General Assembly.

(b) The Commission shall have the authority to apply for, accept, and use any gifts, grants, or financial or other aid, in any form, from the federal government or any agency or instrumentality thereof, or from the State or from any other source including private associations, foundations, or corporations to accomplish any of the duties set out in this Chapter. (1989 (Reg. Sess., 1990), c. 1076, s. 1; 1991 (Reg. Sess., 1992), c. 812, s. 12; c. 816, s. 1; 1993, c. 253, s. 5.1; c. 321, s. 200.1; 1993 (Reg. Sess., 1994), c. 591, s. 6(a); 1995, c. 236, s. 1; 1997-256, s. 6; 1997-347, s. 2; 1997-401, s. 2; 1997-418, s. 2; 1997-443, s. 18.6(a); 1998-202, s. 10(e); 2011-192, s. 8(b).)

§ 164-45. Administrative direction and supervision.

The Commission shall be administered under the direction and supervision of the Director of the Administrative Office of the Courts. The Commission shall exercise all of its prescribed statutory powers independently of the head of that Office, except that all management functions shall be performed under the direction and supervision of the Director of the Administrative Office of the Courts. "Management functions," as used in this section, means planning, organizing, staffing, directing, coordinating, and budgeting. (1989 (Reg. Sess., 1990), c. 1076, s. 1; 1991 (Reg. Sess., 1992), c. 812, s. 12; c. 816, s. 1; 1993, c. 253, s. 5.1; c. 321, s. 200.1; 1993 (Reg. Sess., 1994), c. 591, s. 6(a); 1995, c. 236, s. 1; 1997-256, s. 6; 1997-347, s. 2; 1997-401, s. 2; 1997-418, s. 2; 1997-443, s. 18.6(a).)

§ 164-46: Repealed by Session Laws 1998-212, s. 16.18(b).

§ 164-47. Biennial Report on Recidivism.

The Judicial Department, through the North Carolina Sentencing and Policy Advisory Commission, and the Division of Adult Correction of the Department of Public Safety shall jointly conduct ongoing evaluations of community corrections programs and in-prison treatment programs and make a biennial report to the General Assembly. The report shall include composite measures of program effectiveness based on recidivism rates, other outcome measures, and costs of the programs.

During the 1998-99 fiscal year, the Sentencing and Policy Advisory Commission shall coordinate the collection of all data necessary to create an expanded database containing offender information on prior convictions, current conviction and sentence, program participation, and outcome measures. Each program to be evaluated shall assist the Commission in the development of systems and collection of data necessary to complete the evaluation process. The first evaluation report shall be presented to the Chairs of the Senate and House Appropriations Committees and the Chairs of the Senate and House Appropriations Subcommittees on Justice and Public Safety by April 15, 2000, and future reports shall be made by April 15 of each even-numbered year. (1998-212, s. 16.18(a); 2011-145, s. 19.1(h).)

§ 164-48. Biennial report on juvenile recidivism.

The Judicial Department, through the North Carolina Sentencing and Policy Advisory Commission, shall conduct biennial recidivism studies of juveniles in North Carolina. Each study shall be based upon a sample of juveniles adjudicated delinquent and document subsequent involvement in both the juvenile justice system and criminal justice system for at least two years following the sample adjudication. All State agencies shall provide data as requested by the Commission.

The Sentencing and Policy Advisory Commission shall report the results of the first recidivism study to the Chairs of the Senate and House of Representatives Appropriations Committees and the Chairs of the Senate and House of Representatives Appropriations Subcommittees on Justice and Public Safety by May 1, 2007, and future reports shall be made by May 1 of each odd-numbered year. (2005-276, s. 14.19(a).)

§ 164-49. Biennial report on effectiveness of JCPC grant recipients.

The Judicial Department, through the North Carolina Sentencing and Policy Advisory Commission, shall conduct biennial studies on the effectiveness of programs receiving Juvenile Crime Prevention Council grant funding in North Carolina. Each study shall be based upon a sample of juveniles admitted to programs funded with JCPC grants and document subsequent involvement in both the juvenile justice system and criminal justice system for at least two years following the sample admittance. All State agencies shall provide data as requested by the Commission.

The Sentencing and Policy Advisory Commission shall report the results of the first effectiveness study to the Chairs of the Senate and House of Representatives Appropriations Committees and the Chairs of the Senate and House of Representatives Appropriations Subcommittees on Justice and Public Safety by May 1, 2011, and future reports shall be made by May 1 of each odd-numbered year. (2009-451, s. 15.17J.)

§ 164-50. Annual report on implementation of Justice Reinvestment Project.

The Judicial Department, through the North Carolina Sentencing and Policy Advisory Commission, and the Division of Adult Correction shall jointly conduct ongoing evaluations regarding the implementation of the Justice Reinvestment Act of 2011. The Commission shall present the first evaluation report to the Joint Legislative Correction, Crime Control, and Juvenile Justice Oversight Committee and to the Chairs of the Senate and House of Representatives Appropriations Subcommittees on Justice and Public Safety by April 15, 2012, and future reports shall be made annually by April 15 of each year. (2011-192, s. 8(a); 2011-145, s. 19.1(h).)

Chapter 165.

Veterans.

Article 1.

Department of Administration.

§ 165-1. North Carolina Veterans Commission renamed.

The North Carolina Veterans Commission is hereby renamed the Department of Administration. The Department shall assume all duties, responsibilities and powers formerly exercised by the Veterans Commission, and shall further exercise those powers and duties prescribed in this Article and elsewhere in the General Statutes. (1967, c. 1060, s. 1; 1973, c. 620, s. 9; 1977, c. 70, s. 27.)

§ 165-2. References changed.

Wherever in the General Statutes the words "North Carolina Veterans Commission" appear, the same shall be stricken out and the words "North Carolina Department of Administration" inserted in lieu thereof. (1967, c. 1060, s. 1; 1977, c. 70, s. 27.)

§ 165-3. Definitions.

Wherever used in this Article, unless the context otherwise requires, the terms defined in this section shall have the following meaning:

(1)   "Commission" means the Veterans Affairs Commission.

(2)   "Department" means the North Carolina Department of Administration, an agency of the government of the State of North Carolina.

(3)   Repealed by Session Laws 1973, c. 620, s. 9.

(4)   "Veteran" means

a.   For qualifying as a voting member of the State Board of Veterans Affairs and as the State Director of Veterans Affairs, a person who served honorably during a period of war as defined in Title 38, United States Code.

b.   For entitlement to the services of the Department of Administration, any person who may be entitled to any benefits or rights under the laws of the United States by reason of service in the Armed Forces of the United States.

(5)   "Veterans' organization" means any organization of veterans which has been chartered by an act of the United States Congress and is legally constituted and operating in this State pursuant to said charter. (1945, c. 723, s. 1; 1949, c. 430, s. 1; 1967, c. 1060, s. 1; 1973, c. 620, s. 9; 1977, c. 70, s. 27; 2011-183, s. 112.)

§ 165-4. Purpose.

The purpose of this Article is to provide assistance to veterans, their families and their dependents, in obtaining or maintaining privileges, rights and benefits to which they are entitled under federal, State or local laws. (1945, c. 723, s. 1; 1967, c. 1060, s. 1.)

§ 165-5. Repealed by Session Laws 1973, c. 620, s. 9.

§ 165-6. Powers and duties of the Department.

In furtherance of the stated purpose of this Article, the Department is hereby authorized and empowered to do the following:

(1)   To assist veterans, their families, and dependents in the presentation, processing, proof, and establishment of such claims, privileges, rights, and

benefits as they may be entitled to under federal, State, or local laws, rules, and regulations.

(2)   To aid persons in active military service and their dependents with problems arising out of said service which come reasonably within the purview of the Department's program of assistance.

(3)   To collect data and information as to the facilities and services available to veterans, their families, and dependents and to cooperate with agencies furnishing information or services throughout the State in order to inform such agencies regarding the availability of (i) education, training and retraining facilities, (ii) health, medical, rehabilitation, and housing services and facilities, (iii) employment and reemployment services, (iv) provisions of federal, State, and local laws, rules, and regulations affording rights, privileges, and benefits to veterans, their families, and dependents, and in respect to such other matters of similar, related, or appropriate nature not herein set out.

(4)   To establish such field offices, facilities and services throughout the State as may be necessary to carry out the purposes of this Article.

(5)   To cooperate, as the Department deems appropriate, with governmental, private and civic agencies and instrumentalities in securing services or benefits for veterans, their families, dependents and beneficiaries.

(6)   To accept any property, funds, service, or facilities from any source, public or private, granted in aid or furtherance of the administration of the provisions of this Article.

(7)   To enter into any contract or agreement with any person, firm, or corporation, or governmental agency or instrumentality in furtherance of the purposes of this Article, and to make all rules and regulations necessary for the proper and effective administration of its duties.

(8)   It shall be the duty of the Department to train, assist, and provide guidance to the employees of any county, city, town, or Indian tribe who are engaged in veterans service. Authority is hereby granted the governing body of any county, city or town to appropriate such amounts as it may deem necessary to provide a veterans service program and the expenditure of such funds is hereby declared to be for a public purpose; such program shall be operated in affiliation with this Department as set forth above and in compliance with Department policies and procedures.

(9) The Department may, in its discretion, contribute to each county an amount not to exceed two thousand dollars ($2,000) on a matching basis for any fiscal year for the maintenance and operation of a county veterans service program. Participating counties shall furnish the Department such reports, accountings and other information at such times and in such form as the Department may require.

(10) Repealed by Session Laws 1973, c. 620, s. 9. (1945, c. 723, s. 1; 1949, c. 1292; 1967, c. 1060, s. 1; 1973, c. 620, s. 9; 1985, c. 757, s. 61(a); 2009-280, s. 1.)

§ 165-7. Repealed by Session Laws 1973, c. 620, s. 9.

§ 165-8. Quarters.

The Department of Administration shall provide, in the City of Raleigh, adequate quarters for the central office of the Department of Administration. The Department of Administration shall procure suitable space for its field offices and other activities pursuant to applicable provisions of law and in accordance with rules adopted by the Governor with the approval of the Council of State. (1945, c. 723, s. 1; 1967, c. 1060, s. 1; 1973, c. 620, s. 9; 1977, c. 70, s. 27.)

§ 165-9. Appropriations.

Appropriations for the Department shall be made from the general fund of the State, and the Governor, with the approval of the Council of State, is hereby authorized and empowered to allocate from time to time from the Contingency and Emergency Fund, such funds as may be necessary to carry out the intent and purposes of this Article. (1945, c. 723, s. 1; 1967, c. 1060, s. 1.)

§ 165-10. Transfer of veterans' activities.

The Governor may transfer to the Department such funds, facilities, properties and activities now being held or administered by the State for the benefit of veterans, their families and dependents, as he may deem proper; provided, that the provisions of this section shall not apply to the activities of the Department of

Commerce, Division of Employment Security, in respect to veterans. (1945, c. 723, s. 1; 1967, c. 1060, s. 1; 2011-401, s. 3.25.)

§ 165-11. Copies of records to be furnished to the Department of Administration.

(a)   Whenever copies of any State and local public records are requested by a representative of the Department of Administration in assisting persons in obtaining any federal, State, local or privately provided benefits relating to veterans and their beneficiaries, the official charged with the custody of any such records shall without charge furnish said representative with the requested number of certified copies of such records; provided, that this section shall not apply to the disclosure of information in certain privileged and confidential records referred to elsewhere in the General Statutes of North Carolina, which information shall continue to be disclosed in the manner prescribed by the statute relating thereto.

(b)   No official chargeable with the collection of any fee or charge under the laws of the State of North Carolina in connection with his official duties shall be held accountable on his official bond or otherwise for any fee or charge remitted pursuant to the provisions of this section. (1967, c. 1060, s. 1; 1973, c. 620, s. 9; 1977, c. 70, s. 27.)

§ 165-11.1. Confidentiality of Veterans Affairs records.

Notwithstanding any other provisions of Chapter 143B, no records of the Division of Veterans Affairs in the Department of Administration shall be disclosed or used for any purpose except for official purposes, and no records shall be disclosed, destroyed or used in any manner which is in violation of any existing federal law or regulation. Nothing in this Chapter shall convert records which are the property of the federal government into State property. (1977, c. 70, s. 28.)

Article 2.

Minor Veterans.

§ 165-12. Short title.

This Article may be cited as "The Minor Veterans Enabling Act." (1945, c. 770.)

§ 165-13. Definition.

As used in this Article, "veteran" means any person who may be entitled to any benefits or rights under the laws of the United States, by reason of service in the Armed Forces of the United States. (1945, c. 770; 1967, c. 1060, s. 2; 2011-183, s. 113.)

§ 165-14. Application of Article.

This Article applies to every person, either male or female, 18 years of age or over, but under 21 years of age, who is, or who may become, entitled to any rights or benefits under the laws of the United States relating to veterans benefits. (1945, c. 770; 1967, c. 1060, s. 3.)

§ 165-15. Purpose of Article.

The purpose of this Article is to remove the disqualification of age which would otherwise prevent persons to whom this Article applies from taking advantage of any right or benefit to which they may be or may become entitled under the laws of the United States relating to veterans benefits, and to assure those dealing with such minor persons that the acts of such minors shall not be invalid or voidable by reason of the age of such minors, but shall in all respects be as fully binding as if said minors had attained their majority; and this Article shall be liberally construed to accomplish that purpose. (1945, c. 770; 1967, c. 1060, s. 4.)

§ 165-16. Rights conferred; limitation.

(a) Every person to whom this Article applies is hereby authorized and empowered, in his or her own name without order of court or the intervention of any guardian or trustee:

(1) To purchase or lease any property, either real or personal, or both, which such person may deem it desirable to purchase or lease in order to avail himself or herself of any of the benefits of the laws of United States relating to

veterans benefits, and take title to such property in his or her own name or in the name of himself or herself and spouse.

(2) To execute any note or similar instrument for any part or all of the purchase price of any property purchased pursuant to subdivision (1) of this section and to secure the payment thereof by retained title contract, mortgage, deed of trust or other similar or appropriate instrument.

(3) To execute any other contract or instrument which such person may deem necessary in order to enable such person to secure the benefits of the laws of the United States relating to veterans benefits.

(4) To execute any contract or instrument which such person may deem necessary or proper in order to enable such person to make full use of any property purchased pursuant to the provisions of the laws of the United States relating to veterans benefits, including the right to dispose of such property; such contracts to include but not to be limited to the following:

a. With respect to a home: Contracts for insurance, repairs, and services such as gas, water, and lights, and contracts for furniture and other equipment.

b. With respect to a farm: Contracts such as are included in paragraph (a) of this subdivision (4) above, together with contracts for livestock, seeds, fertilizer and farm equipment and machinery, and contracts for farm labor and other farm services.

c. With respect to a business: Contracts such as are included in paragraph (a) of this subdivision (4), together with such other contracts as such person may deem necessary or proper for the maintenance and operation of such business.

(b) Every person to whom this Article applies may execute such contracts as are hereby authorized in his own name without any order from any court, and without the intervention of a guardian or trustee, and no note, mortgage, conveyance, deed of trust, contract, or other instrument, conveyance or action within the purview of this Article shall be invalid, voidable or defective by reason of the fact that the person executing or performing the same was at the time a minor.

(c) In respect to any action at law or special proceeding in relation to any transaction within the purview of this Article, every minor person to whom this

Article applies shall appear and plead in his or her own name and right without the intervention of any guardian or trustee, and every such minor person shall be considered a legal party to any such action at law or special proceeding in all respects as if such person had attained the age of 21 years. No such minor shall hereafter interpose the defense of lack of legal capacity by reason of age in connection with any transaction within the purview of this Article, nor disavow any such transaction upon coming of age.

(d) All such authority and power as are conferred by this Article are subject to all applicable provisions of the laws of the United States relating to veterans benefits. (1945, c. 770; 1967, c. 1060, s. 5.)

Article 3.

Minor Spouses of Veterans.

§ 165-17. Definition.

As used in this Article, "veteran" means any person who may be entitled to any benefits or rights under the laws of the United States, by reason of service in the Armed Forces of the United States. (1945, c. 771; 1967, c. 1060, s. 6; 2011-183, s. 114.)

§ 165-18. Rights conferred.

(a) Any person under the age of 18 years who is the husband or wife of a veteran, is hereby authorized and empowered in his or her own name, and without any order of court or the intervention of a guardian or trustee, to execute any and all contracts, conveyances, and instruments, to take title to property, to defend any action at law, and to do all other acts necessary to make fully available to such veteran, his or her family or dependents, all rights and benefits under the laws of the United States relating to veterans benefits, in as full and ample manner as if such minor husband or wife of such veteran had attained the age of 18 years.

(b) Any person under the age of 18 years, who is the husband or wife of a veteran, is hereby authorized and empowered in his or her own name, and without any order of court or the intervention of a guardian or trustee, to join in the execution of any contract, deed, conveyance or other instrument which may be deemed necessary to enable his or her veteran spouse to make full use of any property purchased pursuant to the provisions of the foregoing subsection, including the right to dispose of such property.

(c)   With respect to any action at law or special proceeding in relation to any transaction within the purview of this Article, every minor person to whom this Article applies shall appear and plead in his or her own name and right without the intervention of any guardian or trustee; and every such minor person shall be considered a legal party to any such action at law or special proceeding in all respects as if such person had attained the age of 18 years. No such minor shall hereafter interpose the defense of lack of legal capacity by reason of age in connection with any transaction within the purview of this Article, nor disavow any such transaction upon coming of age. (1945, c. 771; 1947, c. 905, ss. 1, 2; 1967, c. 1060, s. 7; 1971, c. 1231, s. 1; 1973, c. 1446, s. 12.)

Article 4.

Scholarships for Children of War Veterans.

§ 165-19. Purpose.

In appreciation for the service and sacrifices of North Carolina's war veterans and as evidence of this State's concern for their children, there is hereby continued a revised program of scholarships for said children as set forth in this Article. (1967, c. 1060, s. 8.)

§ 165-20. Definitions.

As used in this Article the terms defined in this section shall have the following meaning:

(1)   "Active federal service" means full-time duty in the Armed Forces other than active duty for training; however, if disability or death occurs while on active duty for training (i) as a direct result of armed conflict or (ii) while engaged in extra-hazardous service, including such service under conditions simulating war, such active duty for training shall be considered as active federal service.

(2)   "Armed Forces" means the United States Army, Navy, Marine Corps, Air Force, and Coast Guard, including their reserve components.

(3) "Child" means a person: (i) under 25 years of age at the time of application for a scholarship, (ii) who is a domiciliary of North Carolina and is a resident of North Carolina when applying for a scholarship, (iii) who has completed high school or its equivalent prior to receipt of a scholarship awarded under this Article, (iv) who has complied with the requirements of the Selective Service System, if applicable, and (v) who further meets one of the following requirements:

a. A person whose veteran parent was a legal resident of North Carolina at the time of said veteran's entrance into that period of service in the Armed Forces during which eligibility is established under G.S. 165-22.

b. A veteran's child who was born in North Carolina and has been a resident of North Carolina continuously since birth. Provided, that the requirement in the preceding sentence as to birth in North Carolina may be waived by the Department of Administration if it is shown to the satisfaction of the Department that the child's mother was a native-born resident of North Carolina and was such resident at the time of her marriage to the veteran and was outside the State temporarily at the time of the child's birth, following which the child was returned to North Carolina within a reasonable period of time where said child has since lived continuously.

c. A person meeting either of the requirements set forth in subdivision (3) a or b above, and who was legally adopted by the veteran prior to said person's reaching the age of 15 years.

(4) "Period of war" and "wartime" shall mean any of the periods or circumstances as defined below:

a. World War I, meaning (i) the period beginning on April 6, 1917 and ending on November 11, 1918, and (ii) in the case of a veteran who served with the Armed Forces in Russia, the period beginning on April 6, 1917 and ending on April 1, 1920.

b. World War II, meaning the period beginning on December 7, 1941 and ending on December 31, 1946.

c. Korean Conflict, meaning the period beginning on June 27, 1950 and ending on January 31, 1955.

d. Vietnam era, meaning the period beginning on August 5, 1964, and ending on May 7, 1975.

d1. Persian Gulf War, meaning the period beginning on August 2, 1990, and ending on the date prescribed by Presidential proclamation or concurrent resolution of the United States Congress.

e. Any period of service in the Armed Forces during which the veteran parent of an applicant for a scholarship under this Article suffered death or disability (i) as a direct result of armed conflict or (ii) while engaged in extra-hazardous service, including such service under conditions simulating war.

(5) "Private educational institution" means any junior college, senior college or university which is operated and governed by private interests not under the control of the federal, State or any local government, which is located within the State of North Carolina, which does not operate for profit, whose curriculum is primarily directed toward the awarding of associate, baccalaureate or graduate degrees, which agrees to the applicable administration and funding provisions of G.S. 165-22.1, of this Article, and which is otherwise approved by the State Board of Veterans Affairs.

(6) "State educational institution" means any constituent institution of The University of North Carolina, or any community college operated under the provisions of Chapter 115D of the General Statutes of North Carolina.

(7) "Veteran" means a person who served as a member of the Armed Forces in active federal service during a period of war and who was separated from the Armed Forces under conditions other than dishonorable. A person who was separated from the Armed Forces under conditions other than dishonorable and whose death or disability was incurred (i) as a direct result of armed conflict or (ii) while engaged in extra-hazardous service, including such service under conditions simulating war, shall also be deemed a "veteran" and such death or disability shall be considered wartime service-connected. (1967, c. 1060, s. 8; 1969, c. 720, s. 3; c. 741, ss. 1, 2; 1971, c. 339; 1973, c. 620, s. 9; c. 755; 1975, c. 160, s. 1; 1977, c. 70, s. 27; 1985, c. 39, s. 2; c. 788; 1989, c. 767, s. 1; 1991, c. 549, s. 1; 2001-424, s. 7.1(a); 2002-126, s. 19.3(a); 2008-107, s. 19.2(b); 2008-187, s. 48; 2008-192, s. 11; 2011-183, s. 115.)

§ 165-21. Scholarship.

(a) A scholarship granted pursuant to this Article shall consist of the following benefits in either a State or private educational institution:

(1) With respect to State educational institutions, unless expressly limited elsewhere in this Article, a scholarship shall consist of:

a. Tuition at the State educational institution.

b. A standard board allowance.

c. A standard room allowance.

d. Matriculation and other institutional fees required to be paid as a condition to remaining in the institution and pursuing the course of study selected.

(2) With respect to private educational institutions, a scholarship shall consist of a monetary allowance as prescribed in G.S. 165-22.1(d).

(3) Only one scholarship may be granted pursuant to this Article with respect to each child and it shall not extend for a longer period than four academic years, which years, however, need not be consecutive.

(4) No educational assistance shall be afforded a child under this Article after the end of an eight-year period beginning on the date the scholarship is first awarded. Those persons who have been granted a scholarship under this Article prior to the effective date of this act shall be entitled to the remainder of their period of scholarship eligibility if used prior to August 1, 2010. Whenever a child is enrolled in an educational institution and the period of entitlement ends while enrolled in a term, quarter or semester, such period shall be extended to the end of such term, quarter or semester, but not beyond the entitlement limitation of four academic years.

(5) A scholarship awarded to a student under this section shall not exceed the cost of attendance at the State educational institution at which the student is enrolled. If a student, who is eligible for a scholarship under this section, also receives a scholarship or other grant covering the cost of attendance at the State educational institution for which the scholarship is awarded, then the amount of the scholarship shall be reduced by an appropriate amount determined by the State educational institution at which the student is enrolled. The scholarship shall be reduced so that the sum of all grants and scholarship

aid covering the cost of attendance received by the student, including the scholarship under this section, shall not exceed the cost of attendance for the State educational institution at which the student is enrolled.

(b) Repealed by Session Laws 2002-126, s. 19.3(b), effective November 1, 2002.

(c) If a child is awarded a scholarship under this Article, the Commission shall notify the recipient by May 1st of the year in which the recipient enrolls in college. (1967, c. 1060, s. 8; 1969, c. 741, s. 3; 1975, c. 137, s. 1; 1989, c. 767, s. 2; 2001-424, s. 7.1(b); 2002-126, s. 19.3(b); 2008-107, s. 19.2(a).)

§ 165-22. Classes or categories of eligibility under which scholarships may be awarded.

A child, as defined in this Article, who falls within the provisions of any eligibility class described below shall, upon proper application be considered for a scholarship, subject to the provisions and limitations set forth for the class under which the child is considered:

(1) Class I-A: Under this class a scholarship shall be awarded to any child whose veteran parent

a. Was killed in action or died from wounds or other causes not due to the parent's own willful misconduct while a member of the Armed Forces during a period of war, or

b. Has died of service-connected injuries, wounds, illness or other causes incurred or aggravated during wartime service in the Armed Forces, as rated by the United States Department of Veterans Affairs.

(2) Class I-B: Under this class a limited scholarship providing only those benefits set forth in G.S. 165-21(1)a and d and 165-21(2) of this Article, shall be awarded to any child whose veteran parent, at the time the benefits pursuant to this Article are sought to be availed of, is or was at the time of his death receiving compensation for a wartime service-connected disability of one hundred percent (100%) as rated by the United States Department of Veterans Affairs. Provided, that if the veteran parent of a recipient under this class should die of his wartime service-connected condition before the recipient shall have utilized all of his scholarship eligibility time, then the North Carolina Department

of Administration shall amend the recipient's award from Class I-B to Class I-A for the remainder of the recipient's eligibility time. The effective date of such an amended award shall be determined by the Department of Administration, but, in no event shall it predate the date of the veteran parent's death.

(3)   Class II: Under this class a scholarship may be awarded to not more than 100 children yearly, each of whose veteran parent, at the time the benefits pursuant to this Article are sought to be availed of:

a.   Is or was at the time of the parent's death receiving compensation for a wartime service-connected disability of twenty percent (20%) or more, but less than one hundred percent (100%), as rated by the United States Department of Veterans Affairs, or

b.   Was awarded a Purple Heart for wounds received as a result of an act of any opposing armed force, as a result of an international terrorist attack, or as a result of military operations while serving as part of a peacekeeping force.

(4)   Class III: Under this class a scholarship may be awarded to not more than 100 children yearly, each of whose veteran parent, at the time the benefits pursuant to this Article are sought to be availed of:

a.   Is or was at the time of his death drawing pension for permanent and total disability, nonservice-connected, as rated by the United States Department of Veterans Affairs.

b.   Is deceased and who does not fall within the provisions of any other eligibility class described in G.S. 165-22(1), (2), (3), (4)a., nor (5).

c.   Served in a combat zone, or waters adjacent to a combat zone, or any other campaign, expedition, or engagement for which the United States Department of Defense authorizes a campaign badge or medal, who does not fall within the provisions of any other class described in G.S. 165-22(1), (2), (3), (4)a., or (5).

(5)   Class IV: Under this class a scholarship as defined in G.S. 165-21 shall be awarded to any child whose parent, while serving honorably as a member of the Armed Forces in active federal service during a period of war, as defined in G.S. 165-20(4), was listed by the United States government as (i) missing in action, (ii) captured in line of duty by a hostile force, or (iii) forcibly detained or interned in line of duty by a foreign government or power. (1967, c. 1060, s. 8;

1973, cc. 197, 577; c. 620, s. 9; 1975, c. 160, s. 2; c. 167, s. 1; 1977, c. 70, s. 27; 1989, c. 767, ss. 3, 4; 1991, c. 549, s. 2; 2002-126, s. 19.3(c); 2011-183, s. 116.)

§ 165-22.1. Administration and funding.

(a)   The administration of the scholarship program shall be vested in the Department of Administration, and the disbursing and accounting activities required shall be a responsibility of the Department of Administration. The Veterans Affairs Commission shall determine the eligibility of applicants, select the scholarship recipients, establish the effective date of scholarships, and may suspend or revoke scholarships if the said Veterans Affairs Commission finds that the recipient does not comply with the registration requirements of the Selective Service System or does not maintain an adequate academic status, or if the recipient engages in riots, unlawful demonstrations, the seizure of educational buildings, or otherwise engages in disorderly conduct, breaches of the peace or unlawful assemblies. The Department of Administration shall maintain the primary and necessary records, and the Veterans Affairs Commission shall promulgate such rules and regulations not inconsistent with the other provisions of this Article as it deems necessary for the orderly administration of the program. It may require of State or private educational institutions, as defined in this Article, such reports and other information as it may need to carry out the provisions of this Article. The Department of Administration shall disburse scholarship payments for recipients certified eligible by the Department of Administration upon certification of enrollment by the enrolling institution.

(b)   Funds for the support of this program shall be appropriated to the Department of Administration as a reserve for payment of the allocable costs for room, board, tuition, and other charges, and shall be placed in a separate budget code from which disbursements shall be made. Funds to support the program shall be supported by receipts from the Escheat Fund, as provided by G.S. 116B-7, but those funds may be used only for worthy and needy residents of this State who are enrolled in public institutions of higher education of this State. In the event the said appropriation for any year is insufficient to pay the full amounts allocable under the provisions of this Article, such supplemental sums as may be necessary shall be allocated from the Contingency and Emergency Fund. The method of disbursing and accounting for funds allocated for payments under the provisions of this section shall be in accordance with those standards and procedures prescribed by the Director of the Budget, pursuant to the Executive Budget Act.

(c) Allowances for room and board in State educational institutions shall be at such rate as established by the Secretary of the Department of Administration.

(d) Scholarship recipients electing to attend a private educational institution shall be granted a monetary allowance for each term or other academic period attended under their respective scholarship awards. All recipients under Class I-B scholarship shall receive an allowance at one rate, irrespective of course or institution; all recipients under Classes I-A, II, III and IV shall receive a uniform allowance at a rate higher than for Class I-B, irrespective of course or institution. The amount of said allowances shall be determined by the Director of the Budget and made known prior to the beginning of each fall quarter or semester; provided that the Director of the Budget may change the allowances at intermediate periods when in his judgment such changes are necessary. Disbursements by the State shall be to the private institution concerned, for credit to the account of each recipient attending said institution. The manner of payment to any private institution shall be as prescribed by the Department of Administration. The participation by any private institution in the program shall be subject to the applicable provisions of this Article and to examination by State auditors of the accounts of scholarship recipients attending or having attended private institutions. The Veterans Affairs Commission may defer making an award or may suspend an award in any private institution which does not comply with the provisions of this Article relating to said institutions.

(e) Irrespective of other provisions of this Article, the Veterans Affairs Commission may prescribe special procedures for adjusting the accounts of scholarship recipients who for reasons of illness, physical inability to attend class or for other valid reason satisfactory to the Veterans Affairs Commission may withdraw from State or private educational institutions prior to the completion of the term, semester, quarter or other academic period being attended at the time of withdrawal. Such procedures may include, but shall not be limited to, paying the recipient the dollar value of his unused entitlements for the academic period being attended, with a corresponding deduction of this period from his remaining scholarship eligibility time. (1967, c. 1060, s. 8; 1969, c. 720, ss. 4, 5; c. 741, s. 4; 1971, c. 458; 1973, c. 620, s. 9; 1975, c. 19, s. 71; c. 160, s. 3; 1977, c. 70, s. 27; 1985, c. 39, s. 3; 2002-126, s. 19.3(d); 2003-284, s. 18.5(a).)

Article 5.

Veterans' Recreation Authorities.

§ 165-23. Short title.

This Article may be referred to as the "Veterans' Recreation Authorities Law." (1945, c. 460, s. 1.)

§ 165-24. Finding and declaration of necessity.

It is hereby declared that conditions resulting from the concentration in various cities and towns of the State having a population of more than one hundred thousand inhabitants of persons serving in the Armed Forces of the United States in connection with the present war, or who after having served in the Armed Forces of the United States during the present war, or previously have been honorably discharged, require the construction, maintenance and operation of adequate recreation facilities for the use of such persons; that it is in the public interest that adequate recreation facilities be provided in such concentrated centers; and the necessity, in the public interest, for the provisions hereinafter enacted is hereby declared as a matter of legislative determination. (1945, c. 460, s. 2; 2011-183, s. 117.)

§ 165-25. Definitions.

The following terms, wherever used or referred to in this Article, shall have the following respective meanings, unless a different meaning clearly appears from the context:

(1) "Authority" or "recreation authority" shall mean a public body and a body corporate and politic organized in accordance with the provisions of this Article for the purposes, with the powers and subject to the restrictions hereinafter set forth.

(2) "City" shall mean the city or town having a population of more than one hundred thousand inhabitants (according to the last federal census) which is, or is about to be, included in the territorial boundaries of an authority when created hereunder.

(3) "City clerk" and "mayor" shall mean the clerk and mayor, respectively, of the city or the officers thereof charged with the duties customarily imposed on the clerk and mayor, respectively.

(4) "Commissioner" shall mean one of the members of an authority appointed in accordance with the provisions of this Article.

(5) "Council" shall mean the legislative body, council, board of commissioners, board of trustees, or other body charged with governing the city.

(6) "Federal government" shall include the United States of America, the Federal Emergency Administration of Public Works or any agency, instrumentality, corporate or otherwise, of the United States of America.

(7) "Government" shall include the State and federal governments and any subdivision, agency or instrumentality, corporate or otherwise, of any of them.

(8) "Real property" shall include lands, lands under water, structures, and any and all easements, franchises and incorporeal hereditaments and every estate and right therein, legal and equitable, including terms for years and liens by way of judgment, mortgage or otherwise.

(9) "State" shall mean the State of North Carolina.

(10) "Veteran" shall include every person who has enlisted or who has been inducted, warranted or commissioned, and who served honorably in active duty in the military service of the United States at any time, and who is honorably separated or discharged from such service, or who, at the time of making use of the facilities, is still in active service, or has been retired, or who has been furloughed to a reserve. This definition shall be liberally construed, with a view completely to effectuate the purpose and intent of this Article.

(11) "Veterans' recreation project" shall include all real and personal property, buildings and improvements, offices and facilities acquired or constructed, or to be acquired or constructed, pursuant to a single plan or undertaking to provide recreation facilities for veterans in concentrated centers of population. The term "veterans' recreation project" may also be applied to the planning of the buildings and improvements, the acquisition of property, the construction, reconstruction, alteration and repair of the improvements, and all other work in connection therewith. (1945, c. 460, s. 3; 2011-183, s. 118.)

§ 165-26. Creation of authority.

If the council of any city in the State having a population of more than one hundred thousand, according to the last federal census, shall, upon such investigation as it deems necessary, determine:

(1)   That there is a lack of adequate veterans' recreation facilities and accommodations from the operations of public or private enterprises in the city and surrounding area; and/or

(2)   That the public interest requires the construction, maintenance or operation of a veterans' recreation project for the veterans thereof, the council shall adopt a resolution so finding (which need not go into any detail other than the mere finding), and shall cause notice of such determination to be given to the mayor, who shall thereupon appoint, as hereinafter provided, five commissioners to act as an authority. Said Commission shall be a public body and a body corporate and politic upon the completion of the taking of the following proceedings:

The commissioners shall present to the Secretary of State an application signed by them, which shall set forth (without any detail other than the mere recital): (i) that the council has made the aforesaid determination after such investigation, and that the mayor has appointed them as commissioners; (ii) the name and official residence of each of the commissioners, together with a certified copy of the appointment evidencing their right to office, the date and place of induction into and taking oath of office, and that they desire the recreation authority to become a public body and a body corporate and politic under this Article; (iii) the term of office of each of the commissioners; (iv) the name which is proposed for the corporation; and (v) the location and the principal office of the proposed corporation. The application shall be subscribed and sworn to by each of the said commissioners before an officer authorized by the laws of the State to take and certify oaths, who shall certify upon the application that he personally knows the commissioners and knows them to be the officers as asserted in the application, and that each subscribed and swore thereto in the officer's presence. The Secretary of State shall examine the application, and if he finds that the name proposed for the corporation is not identical with that of a person or of any other corporation of this State or so nearly similar as to lead to confusion and uncertainty, he shall receive and file it and shall record it in an appropriate book of record in his office.

When the application has been made, filed and recorded, as herein provided, the authority shall constitute a public body and a body corporate and politic under the name proposed in the application; the Secretary of State shall make and issue to the said commissioners a certificate of incorporation pursuant to this Article, under the seal of the State, and shall record the same with the application.

The boundaries of such authority shall include said city and the area within 10 miles from the territorial boundaries of said city, but in no event shall it include the whole or a part of any other city nor any area included within the boundaries of another authority. In case an area lies within 10 miles of the boundaries of more than one city, such area shall be deemed to be within the boundaries of the authority embracing such area which was first established, all priorities to be determined on the basis of the time of the issuance of the aforesaid certificates by the Secretary of State. After the creation of an authority, the subsequent existence within its territorial boundaries of more than one city shall in no way affect the territorial boundaries of such authority.

In any suit, action or proceeding involving the validity or enforcement of or relating to any contract of the authority, the authority shall be conclusively deemed to have been established in accordance with the provisions of this Article upon proof of the issuance of the aforesaid certificate by the Secretary of State. A copy of such certificate, duly certified by the Secretary of State, shall be admissible evidence in any such suit, action or proceeding, and shall be conclusive proof of the filing and contents thereof. (1945, c. 460, s. 4.)

§ 165-27. Appointment, qualifications and tenure of commissioners.

An authority shall consist of five commissioners appointed by the mayor, and he shall designate the first chairman.

Of the commissioners who are first appointed, two shall serve for a term of one year, two for a term of three years, and one for a term of five years, and thereafter, the terms of office for all commissioners shall be five years. A commissioner shall hold office until his successor has been appointed and qualified. Vacancies shall be filled for the unexpired term. Vacancies occurring by expiration of office or otherwise shall be filled in the following manner: The mayor and the remaining commissioners shall have a joint session and shall unanimously select the person to fill the vacancy; but if they are unable to do so, then such fact shall be certified to the resident judge of the superior court of the

County in which the authority is located, and he shall fill the vacancy. The mayor shall file with the city clerk a certificate of the appointment or reappointment of any commissioner, and such certificate shall be conclusive evidence of the due and proper appointment of such commissioner. A commissioner shall receive no compensation for his services, but he shall be entitled to the necessary expenses, including traveling expenses, incurred in the discharge of his duties.

When the office of the first chairman of the authority becomes vacant, the authority shall select a chairman from among its members. An authority shall select from among its members a vice-chairman, and it may employ a secretary, technical experts and such other officers, agents and employees, permanent and temporary, as it may require, and shall determine their qualifications, duties, and compensation. An authority may employ its own counsel and legal staff. An authority may delegate to one or more of its agents or employees such powers or duties as it may deem proper. (1945, c. 460, s. 5.)

§ 165-28. Duty of the authority and commissioners of the authority.

The authority and its commissioners shall be under a statutory duty to comply or to cause compliance strictly with all provisions of this Article and the laws of the State and in addition thereto, with each and every term, provision and covenant in any contract of the authority on its part to be kept or performed.

The commissioners may, in the exercise of their discretion, limit the use of recreational centers under their control in whole or in part to veterans of one sex. They shall have the authority to make rules and regulations regarding the use of the recreational centers and other matters and things coming within their jurisdiction.

They shall have the authority to appoint one or more advisory committees consisting of representatives of various veterans' organizations and others and may delegate to such committee or committees authority to execute the policies and programs of activity adopted by the commissioners. (1945, c. 460, s. 6; 1965, c. 367.)

§ 165-29. Interested commissioners or employees.

No commissioner or employee of any authority shall acquire any interest, direct or indirect, in any veterans' recreation project or in any property included or planned to be included in any project, nor shall he have any interest, direct or indirect, in any contract or proposed contract for materials or services to be furnished or used in connection with any such project. If any commissioner or employee of an authority owns or controls an interest, direct or indirect, in any property included or planned to be included in any veterans' recreation project, he shall immediately disclose the same in writing to the authority and such disclosure shall be entered upon the minutes of the authority. Failure so to disclose such interest shall constitute misconduct in office. (1945, c. 460, s. 7.)

§ 165-30. Removal of commissioners.

The mayor may remove a commissioner for inefficiency or neglect of duty or misconduct in office, but only after the commissioner shall have been given a copy of the charges against him (which may be made by the mayor) at least 10 days prior to the hearing thereon and had an opportunity to be heard in person or by counsel.

If, after due and diligent search, a commissioner to whom charges are required to be delivered hereunder cannot be found within the county where the authority is located, such charges shall be deemed served upon such commissioner if mailed to him at his last known address as same appears upon the records of the authority.

In the event of the removal of any commissioner, the mayor shall file in the office of the city clerk a record of the proceedings, together with the charges made against the commissioner removed, and the findings thereon. (1945, c. 460, s. 8.)

§ 165-31. Powers of authority.

An authority shall constitute a public body and a body corporate and politic, exercising public powers, and having all the powers necessary or convenient to carry out and effectuate the purposes and provisions of this Article, including the following powers in addition to others herein granted:

To sue and be sued in any court; to make, use and alter a common seal; to purchase, acquire by devise, hold and convey real and personal property; to elect and appoint, in such manner as it determines to be proper, all necessary officers and agents, fix their compensation and define their duties and obligations; to make bylaws and regulations consistent with the laws of the State, for its own government and for the due and orderly conduct of its affairs and management of its property; without limiting the generality of the foregoing, to do any and everything that may be useful and necessary in order to provide recreation for veterans. (1945, c. 460, s. 9; 2011-284, s. 125.)

§ 165-32. Zoning and building laws.

All recreation projects of an authority shall be subject to the planning, zoning, sanitary and building laws, ordinances and regulations applicable to the locality in which the recreation project is situated. (1945, c. 460, s. 10.)

§ 165-33. Tax exemptions.

The authority shall be exempt from the payment of any taxes or fees to the State or any subdivisions thereof, or to any officer or employee of the State or any subdivision thereof. The property of an authority shall be exempt from all local, municipal and county taxes, and for the purpose of such tax exemption, it is hereby declared as a matter of legislative determination that an authority is and shall be deemed to be a municipal corporation. (1945, c. 460, s. 11.)

§ 165-34. Reports.

The authority shall, at least once a year, file with the mayor of the city an audit report by a certified public accountant of its activities for the preceding year, and shall make any recommendations with reference to any additional legislation or other action that may be necessary in order to carry out the purposes of this Article. (1945, c. 460, s. 12.)

§ 165-35. Exemption from Local Government and County Fiscal Control Acts.

The authority shall be exempt from the operation and provisions of Chapter 60 of the Public Laws of North Carolina of 1931, known as the "Local Government Act," and the amendments thereto, and from Chapter 146 of the Public Laws of North Carolina of 1927, known as the "County Fiscal Control Act" and the amendments thereto. (1945, c. 460, s. 13.)

§ 165-36. Conveyance, lease or transfer of property by a city or county to an authority.

Any city or county, in order to provide for the construction, reconstruction, improvement, repair or management of any veterans' recreation project, or in order to accomplish any of the purposes of this Article, may, with or without consideration or for a nominal consideration, lease, sell, convey or otherwise transfer to an authority within the territorial boundaries of which such city or county it is wholly or partly located, any real, personal or mixed property, and in connection with any such transaction, the authority involved may accept such lease, transfer, assignment and conveyance, and bind itself to the performance and observation of any agreements and conditions attached thereto. Any city or county may purchase real property and convey or cause same to be conveyed to an authority. (1945, c. 460, s. 14.)

§ 165-37. Contracts, etc., with federal government.

In addition to the powers conferred upon the authority by other provisions of this Article, the authority is empowered to borrow money and/or accept grants from the federal government for or in aid of the construction of any veterans' recreation project which such authority is authorized by this Article to undertake, to take over any land acquired by the federal government for the construction of such a project, to take over, lease or manage any recreation project constructed or owned by the federal government, and to these ends, to enter into such contracts, mortgages, trust indentures, leases and other agreements which the federal government shall have the right to require. It is the purpose and intent of this Article to authorize every authority to do any and all things necessary to secure the financial aid and the cooperation of the federal government in the construction, maintenance and operation of any veterans' recreation project which the authority is empowered by this Article to undertake. (1945, c. 460, s. 15.)

§ 165-38. Article controlling.

Insofar as the provisions of this Article are inconsistent with the provisions of any other law, the provisions of this Article shall be controlling: Provided, that nothing in this Article shall prevent any city or municipality from establishing, equipping and operating a veterans' recreation project, or extending recreation facilities under the provisions of its charter or any general law other than this Article. (1945, c. 460, s. 17.)

Article 6.

Powers of Attorney.

§ 165-39. Validity of acts of agent performed after death of principal.

No agency created by a power of attorney in writing given by a principal who is at the time of execution, or who, after executing such power of attorney, becomes, either (i) a member of the Armed Forces of the United States, or (ii) a person serving as a merchant seaman outside the limits of the United States, included within the several states and the District of Columbia; or (iii) a person outside said limits by permission, assignment or direction of any department or official of the United States government, in connection with any activity pertaining to or connected with the prosecution of any war in which the United States is then engaged, shall be revoked or terminated by the death of the principal, as to the agent or other person who, without actual knowledge or actual notice of the death of the principal, shall have acted or shall act, in good faith, under or in reliance upon such power of attorney or agency, and any action so taken, unless otherwise invalid or unenforceable, shall be binding on the heirs, devisees, or personal representatives of the principal. (1945, c. 980, s. 1; 1995, c. 379, s. 5; 2011-183, s. 119; 2011-284, s. 126.)

§ 165-40. Affidavit of agent as to possessing no knowledge of death of principal.

An affidavit, executed by the attorney in fact or agent, setting forth that he has not or had not, at the time of doing any act pursuant to the power of attorney, received actual knowledge or actual notice of the revocation or termination of the power of attorney, by death or otherwise, or notice of any facts indicating the same, shall, in the absence of fraud, be conclusive proof of the nonrevocation or nontermination of the power at such time. If the exercise of the power requires execution and delivery of any instrument which is recordable under the laws of this State, such affidavit (when authenticated for record in the manner prescribed by law) shall likewise be recordable. (1945, c. 980, s. 2.)

§ 165-41. Report of "missing" not to constitute revocation.

No report or listing, either official or otherwise, of "missing" or "missing in action," as such words are used in military parlance, shall constitute or be interpreted as constituting actual knowledge or actual notice of the death of such principal or notice of any facts indicating the same, or shall operate to revoke the agency. (1945, c. 980, s. 3.)

§ 165-42. Article not to affect provisions for revocation.

This Article shall not be construed so as to alter or affect any provisions for revocation or termination contained in such power of attorney. (1945, c. 980, s. 4.)

Article 7.

Miscellaneous Provisions.

§ 165-43. Protecting status of State employees in Armed Forces, etc.

Any employee of the State of North Carolina, who has been granted a leave of absence for service in either (i) the Armed Forces of the United States; or (ii) the United States Merchant Marine; or (iii) outside the continental United States with the Red Cross, shall, upon return to State employment, if reemployed in the same position and if within the time limits set forth in the leave of absence, receive an annual salary of at least (i) the annual salary the employee was receiving at the time such leave was granted; plus (ii) an amount obtained by multiplying the step increment applicable to the employee's classification as provided in the classification and salary plan for State employees by the number of years of such service, counting a fraction of a year as a year; provided that no such employee shall receive a salary in excess of the top of the salary range applicable to the classification to which such employee is assigned upon return. (1945, c. 220; 2011-183, s. 120.)

§ 165-44. Korean and Vietnam veterans; benefits and privileges.

(a) All benefits and privileges now granted by the laws of this State to veterans of World War I and World War II and their dependents and next of kin are hereby extended and granted to veterans of the Korean Conflict and their dependents and next of kin.

For the purposes of this section, the term "veterans of the Korean Conflict" means those persons serving in the Armed Forces of the United States during the period beginning on June 27, 1950, and ending on January 31, 1955.

(b)   All benefits and privileges now granted by the laws of this State to veterans of World War I, World War II, the Korean Conflict, and their dependents and next of kin are hereby extended and granted to veterans of the Vietnam era and their dependents and next of kin.

For purposes of this section, the term "veterans of the Vietnam era" means those persons serving in the Armed Forces of the United States during the period beginning August 5, 1964, and ending on such date as shall be prescribed by Presidential proclamation or concurrent resolution of the Congress. (1953, c. 215; 1969, c. 720, ss. 1, 2; 2011-183, s. 121.)

§ 165-44.01. Wearing of medals by public safety personnel.

(a)   Uniformed public safety officers may wear military service medals during the business week prior to Veterans Day, Memorial Day, and the Fourth of July, the day of Veterans Day, Memorial Day, and the Fourth of July, and the business day immediately following Veterans Day, Memorial Day, and the Fourth of July.

(b)   The employer of a uniformed public safety officer shall retain the right to prohibit the wearing of military service medals pursuant to this subsection if the employer determines that wearing the military service medals poses a safety hazard to the uniformed public safety officer or to the public. Any prohibition under this subsection shall only be effective if adopted after this section becomes law.

(c)   This section shall be interpreted in accordance with all applicable federal laws and regulations.

(d)   The following definitions shall apply in this section:

(1) Military service medal. - Any medal, badge, ribbon, or other decoration awarded by the active or reserve components of the Armed Forces of the United States or the North Carolina National Guard to members of those forces.

(2) Public safety officer. - An employee of a public safety agency who is a law enforcement officer, a firefighter, or emergency medical services personnel.

(e) Uniformed public safety officers may not cover their badges when wearing military service medals in compliance with this section. (2009-240, s. 1; 2011-183, s. 122.)

Article 7A.

Priority in Employment Assistance for Veterans of the Armed Forces of the United States.

§ 165-44.1. Purpose.

The General Assembly finds and declares that veterans in North Carolina represent a strong, productive part of the workforce of this State and are disadvantaged in their pursuit of civilian employment through their delayed entry into the civilian labor market and that it is only proper and in the public interest and public welfare that veterans be provided priority in programs of employment and job training assistance. (1997-171, s. 1.)

§ 165-44.2. Veteran defined.

For the purposes of this Article, "veteran" means a person who served on active duty (other than for training) in any component of the Armed Forces of the United States for a period of 180 days or more, unless released earlier because of service-connected disability, and who was discharged or released from the Armed Forces of the United States under honorable conditions. (1997-171, s. 1; 2011-183, s. 124.)

§ 165-44.3. Priority defined.

For the purposes of this Article, "priority" for veterans means that eligible veterans who register or otherwise apply for services shall be extended the opportunity to participate in or otherwise receive the services of the covered providers before the providers extend the opportunity or services to other registered applicants. (1997-171, s. 1.)

§ 165-44.4. Coverage defined.

This Article shall apply to any State agency, department and institution, any county, city, or other political subdivision of the State, any board or commission, and any other public or private recipient which:

(1)   Receives federal job training funds provided to the State or job training funds appropriated by the General Assembly; and

(2)   Provides employment and job training assistance programs and services, including but not limited to employability assessments, support services referrals, and vocational and educational counseling. (1997-171, s. 1.)

§ 165-44.5. Priority employment assistance directed.

All covered service providers, as specified in G.S. 165-44.4, shall establish procedures to provide veterans with priority, not inconsistent with existing federal or State law, to participate in employment and job training assistance programs. (1997-171, s. 1.)

§ 165-44.6. Implementation and performance measures.

The North Carolina Commission on Workforce Preparedness shall:

(1)   Issue implementing directives that shall apply to all covered service providers as specified in G.S. 165-44.4, and revise those directives as necessary to accomplish the purpose of this Article.

(2)   Develop measures of service for veterans that will serve as indicators of compliance with the provisions of this Article by all covered service providers.

(3)   Annually publish and submit to the Joint Legislative Commission on Governmental Operations, beginning not later than October 1, 1998, a report

detailing covered providers' compliance with the provisions of this Article. (1997-171, s. 1.)

Article 8.

State Veterans Home.

§ 165-45. Short Title.

This Article may be referred to as the "State Veterans Home Act". (1995, c. 346, s. 1.)

§ 165-46. Establishment.

The State of North Carolina shall construct, maintain, and operate veterans homes for the aged and infirm veterans resident in this State under the administrative authority and control of the Division of Veterans Affairs of the Department of Administration. There is vested in such Division any and all powers and authority that may be necessary to enable it to establish and operate the homes and to issue rules necessary to operate the homes in compliance with applicable State and federal statutes and regulations. (1995, c. 346, s. 1.)

§ 165-47. Exemption from certificate of need.

Any state veterans home established by the Division of Veterans Affairs shall be exempt from the certificate of need requirements as set out in Article 9 of Chapter 131E, or as may be hereinafter enacted. (1995, c. 346, s. 1.)

§ 165-48. North Carolina Veterans Home Trust Fund.

(a) Establishment. - A trust fund shall be established in the State treasury, for the Division of Veterans Affairs, to be known as the North Carolina Veterans Home Trust Fund.

(b) Composition. - The trust fund shall consist of all funds and monies received by the Veterans Affairs Commission or the Division of Veterans Affairs from the United States, any federal agency or institution, and any other source, whether as a grant, appropriation, gift, contribution, devise, or individual reimbursement, for the care and support of veterans who have been admitted to a State veterans home.

(c)   Use of Fund. - The trust fund created in subsection (a) of this section shall be used by the Division of Veterans Affairs:

(1)   To pay for the care of veterans in said State veterans homes;

(2)   To pay the general operating expenses of the State veterans homes, including the payment of salaries and wages of officials and employees of said homes; and

(3)   To remodel, repair, construct, modernize, or add improvements to buildings and facilities at the homes.

(d)   Miscellaneous. - The following provisions apply to the trust fund created in subsection (a) of this section:

(1)   All funds deposited and all income earned on the investment or reinvestment of such funds shall be credited to the trust fund.

(2)   Any monies remaining in the trust fund at the end of each fiscal year shall remain on deposit in the State treasury to the credit of the North Carolina Veterans Home Trust Fund.

(3)   Nothing contained herein shall prohibit the establishment and utilization of special agency accounts by the Division of Veterans Affairs, as may be approved by the Veterans Affairs Commission, for the receipt and disbursement of personal funds of the State veterans homes' residents or for receipt and disbursement of charitable contributions for use by and for residents. (1995, c. 346, s. 1; 2011-284, s. 127.)

§ 165-49. Funding.

(a)   The Division of Veterans Affairs of the Department of Administration may apply for and receive federal aid and assistance from the United States Department of Veterans Affairs or any other agency of the United States Government authorized to pay federal aid to states for the construction and acquisition of veterans homes under Title 38, United States Code, section 8131 et seq., or for the care or support of disabled veterans in State veterans homes under Title 38, United Stated Code, section 1741 et seq., or from any other federal law for said purposes.

(b)   The Division of Veterans Affairs may receive from any source any gift, contribution, devise, or individual reimbursement, the receipt of which does not exclude any other source of revenue.

(c)   All funds received by the Division shall be deposited in the North Carolina Veterans Home Trust Fund, except for any funds deposited into special agency accounts established pursuant to G.S. 165-48(d)(3). The Veterans Affairs Commission shall authorize the expenditure of all funds from the North Carolina Veterans Home Trust Fund. The Veterans Affairs Commission may delegate authority to the Assistant Secretary of Veterans Affairs for the expenditure of funds from the North Carolina Veterans Home Trust Fund for operations of the State Veterans Nursing Homes. (1995, c. 346, s. 1; 2001-117, s. 1; 2011-284, s. 128.)

§ 165-50. Contracted operation of homes.

The Veterans Affairs Commission may contract with persons or other nongovernmental entities to operate each State veterans home. Contracts for the procurement of services to manage, administer, and operate any State veterans home shall be awarded on a competitive basis through the solicitation of proposals and through the procedures established by statute and the Division of Purchase and Contract. A contract may be awarded to the vendor whose proposal is most advantageous to the State, taking into consideration cost, program suitability, management plan, excellence of program design, key personnel, corporate or company resources, financial condition of the vendor, experience and past performance, and any other qualities deemed necessary by the Veterans Affairs Commission and set out in the solicitation for proposals. Any contract awarded under this section shall not exceed five years in length. The Veterans Affairs Commission is not required to select or recommend the vendor offering the lowest cost proposal but shall select or recommend the vendor who, in the opinion of the Commission, offers the proposal most advantageous to the veterans and the State of North Carolina. (1995, c. 346, s. 1.)

§ 165-51. Program staff.

The Division shall appoint and fix the salary of an Administrative Officer for the State veterans home program. The Administrative Officer shall be an honorably discharged veteran who has served in active military service in the Armed Forces of the United States for other than training purposes. The Administrative Officer shall direct the establishment of the State veterans home program, coordinate the master planning, land acquisition, and construction of all State veterans homes under the procedures of the Office of State Construction, and oversee the ongoing operation of said veterans homes. The Division may hire any required additional administrative staff to help with administrative and operational responsibilities at each established State veterans home. (1995, c. 346, s. 1; 2001-117, s. 2; 2011-183, s. 125.)

§ 165-52. Admission and dismissal authority.

The Veterans Affairs Commission shall have authority to determine administrative standards for admission and dismissal, as well as the medical conditions, of all persons admitted to and dismissed from any State veterans home, and to issue any necessary rules, subject to the requirements set out in G.S. 165-53. (1995, c. 346, s. 1.)

§ 165-53. Eligibility and priorities.

(a)   To be eligible for admission to a State veterans home, an applicant shall meet the following requirements:

(1)   The veteran shall have served in the active Armed Forces of the United States for other than training purposes;

(2)   The veteran shall have been discharged from the Armed Forces of the United States under honorable conditions;

(3)   The veteran shall be disabled by age, disease, or other reason as determined through a physical examination by a State veterans home physician; and

(4)   The veteran shall have resided in the State of North Carolina for two years immediately prior to the date of application.

(b) Eligible veterans will be admitted into a State veterans home or place on waiting lists for admission into a home according to the following priorities:

(1) Eligible wartime veterans will receive priority over eligible nonwartime veterans and will be admitted to the first available bed capable of providing the level of care required. Eligible wartime veterans with equal care requirements will be ranked in chronological order based on the earliest date of receipt of the veteran's application for care.

(2) All other eligible veterans will be ranked in chronological order based on the earliest date of receipt of the veteran's application for care. If more than one application is received on the same date, the Administrative Officer will determine their sequential order on the list according to medical need.

(c) Nonveterans may occupy no more than twenty-five percent (25%) of the total beds in a State veterans home. When any space is available for nonveterans, priority will be established for the following relatives of eligible veterans in the following order:

(1) Spouse.

(2) Widow or widower whose spouse, if living, would be an eligible veteran.

(3) Gold Star parents, defined as the mother or father of a veteran who died an honorable death while in active service to the United States during time of war or emergency. (1995, c. 346, s. 1; 2001-117, s. 3; 2011-183, s. 126.)

§ 165-54. Deposit required.

Each resident of any State veterans home shall pay to the Division of Veterans Affairs the cost of maintaining his or her residence at the home. This deposit shall be placed in the North Carolina Veterans Home Trust Fund and shall be in an amount and in the form prescribed by the Veterans Affairs Commission in consultation with the Assistant Secretary for Veterans Affairs. (1995, c. 346, s. 1.)

§ 165-55. Report and budget.

(a) The Assistant Secretary for Veterans Affairs shall report annually to the Secretary of the Department of Administration on the activities of the State Veterans Homes Program. This report shall contain an accounting of all monies received and expended, statistics on residents in the homes during the year, recommendations to the Secretary, the Governor, and the General Assembly as to the program, and such other matters as may be deemed pertinent.

(b) The Assistant Secretary for Veterans Affairs, with the approval of the Veterans Affairs Commission, shall compile an annual budget request for any State funding needed for the anticipated costs of the homes, which shall be submitted to the Secretary of the Department of Administration. State appropriated funds for operational needs shall be made available only in the event that other sources are insufficient to cover essential operating costs. (1995, c. 346, s. 1.)

Chapter 166

Civil Preparedness Agencies.

§§ 166-1 through 166-13: Repealed by Session Laws 1977, c. 848, s. 1.

Chapter 166A

North Carolina Emergency Management Act.

Article 1.

North Carolina Emergency Management Act of 1977.

§§ 166A-1: Repealed by Session Laws 2012-12, s. 1(a), effective October 1, 2012.

§§ 166A-2: Repealed by Session Laws 2012-12, s. 1(a), effective October 1, 2012.

§§ 166A-3: Repealed by Session Laws 2012-12, s. 1(a), effective October 1, 2012.

§§ 166A-4: Repealed by Session Laws 2012-12, s. 1(a), effective October 1, 2012.

§§ 166A-5: Repealed by Session Laws 2012-12, s. 1(a), effective October 1, 2012.

§§ 166A-6: Repealed by Session Laws 2012-12, s. 1(a), effective October 1, 2012.

§§ 166A-6.01: Repealed by Session Laws 2012-12, s. 1(a), effective October 1, 2012.

§§ 166A-6.02: Repealed by Session Laws 2012-12, s. 1(a), effective October 1, 2012.

§§ 166A-6.03: Repealed by Session Laws 2012-12, s. 1(a), effective October 1, 2012.

§ 166A-6.1: Recodified as G.S. 166A-29 by Session Laws 2012-12, s. 1(a), effective October 1, 2012.

§ 166A-7: Repealed by Session Laws 2012-12, s. 1(a), effective October 1, 2012.

§ 166A-8: Repealed by Session Laws 2012-12, s. 1(a), effective October 1, 2012.

§ 166A-9: Repealed by Session Laws 2012-12, s. 1(a), effective October 1, 2012.

§ 166A-10: Repealed by Session Laws 2012-12, s. 1(a), effective October 1, 2012.

§ 166A-11: Repealed by Session Laws 2012-12, s. 1(a), effective October 1, 2012.

§ 166A-12: Repealed by Session Laws 2012-12, s. 1(a), effective October 1, 2012.

§ 166A-13: Repealed by Session Laws 2012-12, s. 1(a), effective October 1, 2012.

§ 166A-14: Repealed by Session Laws 2012-12, s. 1(a), effective October 1, 2012.

§ 166A-15: Repealed by Session Laws 2012-12, s. 1(a), effective October 1, 2012.

§ 166A-15.1: Repealed by Session Laws 2012-12, s. 1(a), effective October 1, 2012.

§ 166A-16: Repealed by Session Laws 2012-12, s. 1(a), effective October 1, 2012.

§ 166A-17: Repealed by Session Laws 2012-12, s. 1(a), effective October 1, 2012.

§ 166A-18: Repealed by Session Laws 2012-12, s. 1(a), effective October 1, 2012.

Article 1A.

North Carolina Emergency Management Act.

Part 1. General Provisions.

§ 166A-19. Short title.

This Article may be cited as "North Carolina Emergency Management Act." (1977, c. 848, s. 2; 1979, 2nd Sess., c. 1310, s. 2; 1995, c. 509, s. 120; 2012-12, s. 1(b).)

§ 166A-19.1. Purposes.

The purposes of this Article are to set forth the authority and responsibility of the Governor, State agencies, and local governments in prevention of, preparation for, response to, and recovery from natural or man-made emergencies or hostile military or paramilitary action and to do the following:

(1)   Reduce vulnerability of people and property of this State to damage, injury, and loss of life and property.

(2)   Prepare for prompt and efficient rescue, care, and treatment of threatened or affected persons.

(3)   Provide for the rapid and orderly rehabilitation of persons and restoration of property.

(4)   Provide for cooperation and coordination of activities relating to emergency mitigation, preparedness, response, and recovery among agencies and officials of this State and with similar agencies and officials of other states, with local and federal governments, with interstate organizations, and with other private and quasi-official organizations. (1959, c. 337, s. 1; 1975, c. 734, s. 1; 1977, c. 848, s. 2; 1995, c. 509, s. 121; 2012-12, s. 1(b).)

§ 166A-19.2. Limitations.

Nothing in this Article shall be construed to do any of the following:

(1)   Interfere with dissemination of news or comment on public affairs; but any communications facility or organization, including, but not limited to, radio and television stations, wire services, and newspapers may be requested to transmit or print public service messages furnishing information or instructions in connection with an emergency, disaster, or war.

(2)   Limit, modify, or abridge the authority of the Governor to declare martial law or exercise any other powers vested in the Governor under the North Carolina Constitution, statutes, or common law of this State independent of, or in conjunction with, any provisions of this Article. (1975, c. 734, s. 2; 1977, c. 848, s. 2; 1995, c. 509, s. 122; 2012-12, s. 1(b).)

§ 166A-19.3. Definitions.

The following definitions apply in this Article:

(1)   Account. - The State Emergency Response Account established in G.S. 166A-19.42.

(2)   Chair of the board of county commissioners. - The chair of the board of county commissioners or, in case of the chair's absence or disability, the person authorized to act in the chair's stead. Unless the governing body of the county

has specified who is to act in lieu of the chair with respect to a particular power or duty set out in this Article, this term shall mean the person generally authorized to act in lieu of the chair.

(3) Disaster declaration. - A gubernatorial declaration that the impact or anticipated impact of an emergency constitutes a disaster of one of the types enumerated in G.S. 166A-19.21(b).

(4) Division. - The Division of Emergency Management established in Subpart A of Part 5 of Article 13 of Chapter 143B of the General Statutes.

(5) Eligible entity. - Any political subdivision. The term also includes an owner or operator of a private nonprofit utility that meets the eligibility criteria set out in this Article.

(6) Emergency. - An occurrence or imminent threat of widespread or severe damage, injury, or loss of life or property resulting from any natural or man-made accidental, military, paramilitary, weather-related, or riot-related cause.

(7) Emergency area. - The geographical area covered by a state of emergency.

(8) Emergency management. - Those measures taken by the populace and governments at federal, State, and local levels to minimize the adverse effect of any type emergency, which includes the never-ending preparedness cycle of planning, prevention, mitigation, warning, movement, shelter, emergency assistance, and recovery.

(9) Emergency management agency. - A State or local governmental agency charged with coordination of all emergency management activities for its jurisdiction.

(10) Hazard risk management. - The systematic application of policies, practices, and resources to the identification, assessment, and control of risk associated with hazards affecting human health and safety and property. Hazard, risk, and cost-benefit analysis are used to support development of risk reduction options, program objectives, and prioritization of issues and resources.

(11) Mayor. - The mayor or other chief executive official of a municipality or, in case of that person's absence or disability, the person authorized to act in that

person's stead. Unless the governing body of the municipality has specified who is to act in lieu of the mayor with respect to a particular power or duty set out in this Article, the term shall mean the person generally authorized to act in lieu of the mayor.

(12) Political subdivision. - Counties and incorporated cities, towns, and villages.

(13) Preliminary damage assessment. - The initial estimate prepared by State, local, or federal emergency management workers used to determine the severity and magnitude of damage caused by an emergency.

(14) Private nonprofit utility. - A utility that would be eligible for federal public assistance disaster funds pursuant to 44 C.F.R. Part 206.

(15) Secretary. - The Secretary of the Department of Public Safety.

(16) Stafford Act. - The Robert T. Stafford Disaster Relief and Emergency Assistance Act, Pub. L. No. 93-288, 88 Stat. 143, codified generally at 42 U.S.C. § 5121, et seq., as amended.

(17) State Acquisition and Relocation Fund. - State funding for supplemental grants to homeowners participating in a federal Hazard Mitigation Grant Program Acquisition and Relocation Program. These grants are used to acquire safe, decent, and sanitary housing by paying the difference between the cost of the home acquired under the federal Hazard Mitigation Grant Program Acquisition and Relocation Program and the cost of a comparable home located outside the 100-year floodplain.

(18) State Emergency Response Team. - The representative group of State agency personnel designated to carry out the emergency management support functions identified in the North Carolina Emergency Operations Plan. The State Emergency Response Team leader shall be the Director of the Division, who shall have authority to manage the Team pursuant to G.S. 166A-19.12(1), as delegated by the Governor. The Team shall consist of the following State agencies:

a. Department of Public Safety.

b. Department of Transportation.

c. Department of Health and Human Services.

d. Department of Environment and Natural Resources.

e. Department of Agriculture and Consumer Services.

f. Any other agency identified in the North Carolina Emergency Operations Plan.

(19) State of emergency. - A finding and declaration by any of the following authorities that an emergency exists:

a. The Governor, acting under the authority of G.S. 166A-19.20.

b. The General Assembly, acting under the authority of G.S. 166A-19.20.

c. The governing body of a municipality or the mayor of a municipality, acting under the authority of G.S. 166A-19.22.

d. The governing body of a county or the chair of the board of commissioners of a county, acting under the authority of G.S. 166A-19.22. (1951, c. 1016, s. 2; 1953, c. 1099, s. 1; 1955, c. 387, s. 1; 1975, c. 734, ss. 4-6, 14; 1977, c. 848, s. 2; 1979, 2nd Sess., c. 1310, s. 2; 1995, c. 509, s. 123; 2001-214, s. 1; 2006-66, ss. 6.5(c), (d); 2009-193, ss. 1, 2; 2009-397, s. 2; 2012-12, s. 1(b); 2012-90, s. 10.)

§ 166A-19.4: Reserved for future codification purposes.

§ 166A-19.5: Reserved for future codification purposes.

§ 166A-19.6: Reserved for future codification purposes.

§ 166A-19.7: Reserved for future codification purposes.

§ 166A-19.8: Reserved for future codification purposes.

§ 166A-19.9: Reserved for future codification purposes.

Part 2. State Emergency Management.

§ 166A-19.10. Powers of the Governor.

(a)   State Emergency Management Program. - The State Emergency Management Program includes all aspects of preparations for, response to, recovery from, and mitigation against war or peacetime emergencies.

(b)   Powers of the Governor. - The Governor is authorized and empowered to do the following:

(1)   To exercise general direction and control of the State Emergency Management Program and to be responsible for carrying out the provisions of this Article, other than those provisions that confer powers and duties exclusively on local governments.

(2)   To make, amend, or rescind the necessary orders, rules, and regulations within the limits of the authority conferred upon the Governor herein, with due consideration of the policies of the federal government.

(3)   To delegate any authority vested in the Governor under this Article and to provide for the subdelegation of any such authority.

(4)   To cooperate and coordinate with the President and the heads of the departments and agencies of the federal government, and with other appropriate federal officers and agencies, and with the officers and agencies of other states and local units of government in matters pertaining to the emergency management of the State and nation.

(5)   To enter into agreements with the American National Red Cross, Salvation Army, Mennonite Disaster Service, and other disaster relief organizations.

(6)   To make, amend, or rescind mutual aid agreements in accordance with G.S. 166A-19.72.

(7)   To utilize the services, equipment, supplies, and facilities of existing departments, offices, and agencies of the State and of the political subdivisions thereof. The officers and personnel of all such departments, offices, and agencies are required to cooperate with and extend such services and facilities to the Governor upon request. This authority shall extend to a state of

emergency declared pursuant to G.S. 166A-19.20, to the imminent threat of an emergency that will likely require an emergency to be declared pursuant to G.S. 166A-19.20, or to emergency management planning and training purposes.

(8) To agree, when required to obtain federal assistance in debris removal, that the State will indemnify the federal government against any claim arising from the removal of the debris.

(9) To sell, lend, lease, give, transfer, or deliver materials or perform services for emergency purposes on such terms and conditions as may be prescribed by any existing law, and to account to the State Treasurer for any funds received for such property.

(10) In an emergency, or when requested by the governing body of a political subdivision in the State, to assume operational control over all or any part of the emergency management functions within this State. (1951, c. 1016, ss. 3, 9; 1953, c. 1099, s. 3; 1955, c. 387, ss. 2, 3, 5; 1957, c. 950, s. 5; 1975, c. 734, ss. 9, 10, 14, 16; 1977, c. 848, s. 2; 1979, 2nd Sess., c. 1310, s. 2; 1995, c. 509, s. 124; 2001-214, s. 2; 2002-179, s. 12; 2009-192, s. 1; 2009-193, s. 3; 2009-196, s. 1; 2009-225, s. 1; 2011-145, s. 19.1(g); 2012-12, s. 1(b).)

§ 166A-19.11. Powers of the Secretary of Public Safety.

The Secretary shall be responsible to the Governor for State emergency management activities. The Secretary shall have the following powers and duties as delegated by the Governor:

(1) To activate the State and local plans applicable to the areas in question and to authorize and direct the deployment and use of any personnel and forces to which the plan or plans apply, and the use or distribution of any supplies, equipment, materials, and facilities available pursuant to this Article or any other provision of law.

(2) To adopt the rules to implement those provisions of this Article that deal with matters other than those that are exclusively local.

(3) To develop a system to produce a preliminary damage assessment from which the Secretary will recommend the appropriate level of disaster declaration to the Governor. The system shall, at a minimum, consider whether the damage

involved and its effects are of such a severity and magnitude as to be beyond the response capabilities of the local government or political subdivision.

(4)   Additional authority, duties, and responsibilities as may be prescribed by the Governor. The Secretary may subdelegate his authority to the appropriate member of the Secretary's department. (1951, c. 1016, ss. 3, 9; 1953, c. 1099, s. 3; 1955, c. 387, ss. 2, 3, 5; 1957, c. 950, s. 5; 1975, c. 734, ss. 9, 10, 14, 16; 1977, c. 848, s. 2; 1979, 2nd Sess., c. 1310, s. 2; 1995, c. 509, s. 124; 2001-214, s. 2; 2002-179, s. 12; 2009-192, s. 1; 2009-193, s. 3; 2009-196, s. 1; 2009-225, s. 1; 2011-145, s. 19.1(g); 2012-12, s. 1(b).)

§ 166A-19.12. Powers of the Division of Emergency Management.

The Division of Emergency Management shall have the following powers and duties as delegated by the Governor and Secretary of Public Safety:

(1)   Coordination of the activities of all State agencies for emergency management within the State, including planning, organizing, staffing, equipping, training, testing, and activating and managing the State Emergency Response Team and emergency management programs.

(2)   Preparation and maintenance of State plans for emergencies. The State plans or any parts thereof may be incorporated into department regulations and into executive orders of the Governor.

(3)   Coordination with the State Health Director to amend or revise the North Carolina Emergency Operations Plan regarding public health matters. At a minimum, the revisions to the Plan shall provide for the following:

a.   The epidemiologic investigation of a known or suspected threat caused by nuclear, biological, or chemical agents.

b.   The examination and testing of persons and animals that may have been exposed to a nuclear, biological, or chemical agent.

c.   The procurement and allocation of immunizing agents and prophylactic antibiotics.

d.   The allocation of the Strategic National Stockpile.

e. The appropriate conditions for quarantine and isolation in order to prevent further transmission of disease.

f. Immunization procedures.

g. The issuance of guidelines for prophylaxis and treatment of exposed and affected persons.

(4) Establishment of a voluntary model registry for use by political subdivisions in identifying functionally and medically fragile persons in need of assistance during an emergency. All records, data, information, correspondence, and communications relating to the registration of persons with special needs or of functionally and medically fragile persons obtained pursuant to this subdivision are confidential and are not a public record pursuant to G.S. 132-1 or any other applicable statute, except that this information shall be available to emergency response agencies, as determined by the local emergency management director. This information shall be used only for the purposes set forth in this subdivision.

(5) Promulgation of standards and requirements for local plans and programs consistent with federal and State laws and regulations, determination of eligibility for State financial assistance provided for in G.S. 166A-19.15, and provision of technical assistance to local governments. Standards and requirements for local plans and programs promulgated under this subdivision shall be reviewed by the Division at least biennially and updated as necessary.

(6) Development and presentation of training programs, including the Emergency Management Certification Program established under Article 5 of this Chapter, and public information programs to insure the furnishing of adequately trained personnel and an informed public in time of need.

(7) Making of such studies and surveys of the resources in this State as may be necessary to ascertain the capabilities of the State for emergency management, maintaining data on these resources, and planning for the most efficient use thereof.

(8) Coordination of the use of any private facilities, services, and property.

(9) Preparation for issuance by the Governor of executive orders, declarations, and regulations as necessary or appropriate.

(10) Cooperation and maintenance of liaison with the other states, the federal government, and any public or private agency or entity in achieving any purpose of this Article and in implementing programs for emergency or war prevention, preparation, response, and recovery.

(11) Making recommendations, as appropriate, for zoning, building, and other land-use controls, and safety measures for securing mobile homes or other nonpermanent or semipermanent works designed to protect against or mitigate the effects of an emergency.

(12) Coordination of the use of existing means of communications and supplementing communications resources and integrating them into a comprehensive State or State-federal telecommunications or other communications system or network.

(13) Administration of federal and State grant funds provided for emergency management purposes, including those funds provided for planning and preparedness activities by emergency management agencies.

(14) Serving as the lead State agency for the coordination of information and resources for hazard risk management, which shall include the following responsibilities:

a. Coordinating with other State agencies and county governments in conducting hazard risk analysis. To the extent another State agency has primary responsibility for the adoption of hazard mitigation standards, those standards shall be applied in conducting a hazard risk analysis.

b. Establishing and maintaining a hazard risk management information system and tools to display natural hazards and vulnerabilities and conducting risk assessment.

c. Acquiring and leveraging all natural hazard data generated or maintained by State agencies and county governments.

d. Acquiring and leveraging all vulnerability data generated or maintained by State agencies and county governments.

e. Maintaining a clearinghouse for methodologies and metrics for calculating and communicating hazard probability and loss estimation.

(15) Utilizing and maintaining technology that enables efficient and effective communication and management of resources between political subdivisions, State agencies, and other governmental entities involved in emergency management activities.

(16) Establishing and operating a 24-hour Operations Center to serve as a single point of contact for local governments to report the occurrence of emergency and disaster events and to coordinate local and State response assets.

(17) Developing, maintaining, and implementing plans for response to any emergency occurring at a fixed nuclear power generating facility located in or near the borders of the State of North Carolina.

(18) Maintaining the State Emergency Operations Center as the facility to house the State Emergency Response Team whenever it is activated for disaster response.

(19) Serving as the agency responsible for the management of intrastate and interstate mutual aid planning, implementation, and resource procurement necessary for supporting emergency response and recovery.

(20) Coordination with the Commissioner of Agriculture, or the Commissioner's designee, to amend or revise the North Carolina Emergency Operations Plan regarding agricultural matters. At a minimum, the revisions to the Plan shall provide for the following:

a. The examination and testing of animals that may have been exposed to a nuclear, biological, or chemical agent.

b. The appropriate conditions for quarantine and isolation of animals in order to prevent further transmission of disease. (1951, c. 1016, ss. 3, 9; 1953, c. 1099, s. 3; 1955, c. 387, ss. 2, 3, 5; 1957, c. 950, s. 5; 1975, c. 734, ss. 9, 10, 14, 16; 1977, c. 848, s. 2; 1979, 2nd Sess., c. 1310, s. 2; 1995, c. 509, s. 124; 2001-214, s. 2; 2002-179, s. 12; 2009-192, s. 1; 2009-193, s. 3; 2009-196, s. 1; 2009-225, s. 1; 2011-145, s. 19.1(g); 2012-12, s. 1(b); 2012-90, ss. 11, 12.)

§ 66A-19.13: Reserved for future codification purposes.

§ 66A-19.14: Reserved for future codification purposes.

Part 3. Local Emergency Management.

§ 166A-19.15. County and municipal emergency management.

(a) Governing Body of Counties Responsible for Emergency Management. - The governing body of each county is responsible for emergency management within the geographical limits of such county. All emergency management efforts within the county will be coordinated by the county, including activities of the municipalities within the county.

(b) Counties May Establish and Maintain Emergency Management Agencies. - The governing body of each county is hereby authorized to establish and maintain an emergency management agency for the purposes contained in G.S. 166A-19.1. The governing body of each county which establishes an emergency management agency pursuant to this authorization shall appoint a coordinator who will have a direct responsibility for the organization, administration, and operation of the county program and will be subject to the direction and guidance of such governing body. In the event that any county fails to establish an emergency management agency, and the Governor, in the Governor's discretion, determines that a need exists for such an emergency management agency, then the Governor is hereby empowered to establish an emergency management agency within that county.

(c) Municipalities May Establish and Maintain Emergency Management Agencies. - All incorporated municipalities are authorized to establish and maintain emergency management agencies subject to coordination by the county.

(d) Joint Agencies Authorized. - Counties and incorporated municipalities are authorized to form joint emergency management agencies composed of a county and one or more municipalities within the county's borders, between two or more counties, or between two or more counties and one or more municipalities within the borders of those counties.

(e) Local Appropriations Authorized. - Each county and incorporated municipality in this State is authorized to make appropriations for the purposes of this Article and to fund them by levy of property taxes pursuant to G.S. 153A-

149 and G.S. 160A-209 and by the allocation of other revenues, use of which is not otherwise restricted by law.

(f) Additional Powers. - In carrying out the provisions of this Article each political subdivision is authorized to do the following:

(1) To appropriate and expend funds, make contracts, obtain and distribute equipment, materials, and supplies for emergency management purposes and to provide for the health and safety of persons and property, including emergency assistance, consistent with this Article.

(2) To direct and coordinate the development of emergency management plans and programs in accordance with the policies and standards set by the Division, consistent with federal and State laws and regulations.

(3) To assign and make available all available resources for emergency management purposes for service within or outside of the physical limits of the subdivision.

(4) To delegate powers in a local state of emergency declared pursuant to G.S. 166A-19.22.

(5) To coordinate the voluntary registration of functionally and medically fragile persons in need of assistance during an emergency either through a registry established by this subdivision or by the State. All records, data, information, correspondence, and communications relating to the registration of persons with special needs or of functionally and medically fragile persons obtained pursuant to this subdivision are confidential and are not a public record pursuant to G.S. 132-1 or any other applicable statute, except that this information shall be available to emergency response agencies, as determined by the local emergency management director. This information shall be used only for the purposes set forth in this subdivision.

(g) County Eligibility for State and Federal Financial Assistance. - Each county which establishes an emergency management agency pursuant to State standards and which meets requirements for local plans and programs may be eligible to receive State and federal financial assistance, including State and federal funding appropriated for emergency management planning and preparedness, and for the maintenance and operation of a county emergency management program. Such financial assistance is subject to an appropriation being made for this purpose. Where the appropriation does not allocate appropriated funds among counties, the amount allocated to each county shall be determined annually by the Division. The size of this allocation shall be based in part on the degree to which local plans and programs meet State standards and requirements promulgated by the Division, including those relating to professional competencies of local emergency management personnel. However, in making an allocation determination, the Division shall, where appropriate, take into account the fact that a particular county may lack sufficient resources to meet the standards and requirements promulgated by the Division. (1951, c. 1016, s. 6; 1953, c. 1099, s. 4; 1957, c. 950, s. 2; 1959, c. 337, s. 5; 1973, c. 620, s. 9; 1975, c. 734, ss. 12, 14, 16; 1977, c. 848, s. 2; 1979, 2nd Sess., c. 1310, s. 2; 1995, c. 509, ss. 126, 127; 2009-196, s. 2; 2009-225, s. 2; 2012-12, s. 1(b).)

§ 166A-19.16: Reserved for future codification purposes.

§ 166A-19.17: Reserved for future codification purposes.

§ 166A-19.18: Reserved for future codification purposes.

§ 166A-19.19: Reserved for future codification purposes.

Part 4. Declarations of State of Emergency.

§ 166A-19.20. Gubernatorial or legislative declaration of state of emergency.

(a) Declaration. - A state of emergency may be declared by the Governor or by a resolution of the General Assembly, if either of these finds that an emergency exists.

(b) Emergency Area. - An executive order or resolution declaring a state of emergency shall include a definition of the area constituting the emergency area.

(c) Expiration of States of Emergency. - A state of emergency declared pursuant to this section shall expire when it is rescinded by the authority that issued it.

(d) Exercise of Powers Not Contingent on Declaration of Disaster Type. - Once a state of emergency has been declared pursuant to this section, the fact that a declaration of disaster type has not been issued shall not preclude the exercise of powers otherwise conferred during a state of emergency. (1951, c. 1016, s. 4; 1955, c. 387, s. 4; 1959, c. 284, s. 2; c. 337, s. 4; 1975, c. 734, ss. 11, 14; 1977, c. 848, s. 2; 1979, 2nd Sess., c. 1310, s. 2; 1993, c. 321, s. 181(a); 1995, c. 509, s. 125; 2001-214, s. 3; 2011-145, s. 19.1(g); 2011-183, s. 127(c); 2012-12, s. 1(b).)

§ 166A-19.21. Gubernatorial disaster declaration.

(a)   Preliminary Damage Assessment. - When a state of emergency is declared pursuant to G.S. 166A-19.20, the Secretary shall provide the Governor and the General Assembly with a preliminary damage assessment as soon as the assessment is available.

(b)   Declaration of Disaster. - Upon receipt of a preliminary damage assessment, the Governor is authorized to issue a disaster declaration declaring the impact or anticipated impact of the emergency to constitute a disaster of one of the following types:

(1)   Type I disaster. - A Type I disaster may be declared by the Governor prior to, and independently of, any action taken by the Small Business Administration, the Federal Emergency Management Agency, or any other federal agency, if all of the following criteria are met:

a.   A local state of emergency has been declared pursuant to G.S. 166A-19.22 and a written copy of the declaration has been forwarded to the Governor.

b.   The preliminary damage assessment meets or exceeds the criteria established for the Small Business Administration Disaster Loan Program pursuant to 13 C.F.R. Part 123 or meets or exceeds the State infrastructure criteria set out in G.S. 166A-19.41(b)(2)a.

c.   A major disaster declaration by the President of the United States pursuant to the Stafford Act has not been declared.

(2)   Type II disaster. - A Type II disaster may be declared if the President of the United States has issued a major disaster declaration pursuant to the Stafford Act. The Governor may request federal disaster assistance under the Stafford Act without making a Type II disaster declaration.

(3) Type III disaster. - A Type III disaster may be declared if the President of the United States has issued a major disaster declaration under the Stafford Act and either of the following is true:

a. The preliminary damage assessment indicates that the extent of damage is reasonably expected to meet the threshold established for an increased federal share of disaster assistance under applicable federal law and regulations.

b. The preliminary damage assessment prompts the Governor to call a special session of the General Assembly to establish programs to meet the unmet needs of individuals, businesses, or political subdivisions affected by the emergency.

(c) Expiration of Disaster Declarations. -

(1) Expiration of Type I disaster declarations. - A Type I disaster declaration shall expire 60 days after its issuance unless renewed by the Governor or the General Assembly. Such renewals may be made in increments of 30 days each, not to exceed a total of 120 days from the date of first issuance. The Joint Legislative Commission on Governmental Operations shall be notified prior to the issuance of any renewal of a Type I disaster declaration.

(2) Expiration of Type II disaster declarations. - A Type II disaster declaration shall expire twelve months after its issuance unless renewed by the Governor or the General Assembly. Such renewals may be made in increments of three months each. A Type II disaster declaration and any renewals of that declaration shall not exceed a total of 24 months. The Joint Legislative Commission on Governmental Operations shall be notified prior to the issuance of any renewal of a Type II disaster declaration.

(3) Expiration of Type III disaster declarations. - A Type III disaster declaration shall expire 24 months after its issuance unless renewed by the General Assembly.

(4) Expiration of disaster declarations declared prior to July 1, 2001. - Any state of disaster declared or proclaimed before July 1, 2001, irrespective of type, shall terminate by a declaration of the Governor or resolution of the General Assembly. A declaration or resolution declaring or terminating a state of disaster shall be disseminated promptly by means calculated to bring its contents to the attention of the general public and, unless the circumstances attendant upon the

disaster prevent or impede, promptly filed with the Secretary, the Secretary of State, and the clerks of superior court in the area to which it applies.

(d) Effect of Disaster Declaration Expiration. - Expiration of a Type II or III disaster declaration shall not affect the State's obligations under federal-State agreements entered into prior to the expiration of the disaster declaration. (1951, c. 1016, s. 4; 1955, c. 387, s. 4; 1959, c. 284, s. 2; c. 337, s. 4; 1975, c. 734, ss. 11, 14; 1977, c. 848, s. 2; 1979, 2nd Sess., c. 1310, s. 2; 1993, c. 321, s. 181(a); 1995, c. 509, s. 125; 2001-214, s. 3; 2011-145, s. 19.1(g); 2011-183, s. 127(c); 2012-12, s. 1(b); 2012-90, ss. 7, 8.)

§ 166A-19.22. Municipal or county declaration of state of emergency.

(a) Declaration. - A state of emergency may be declared by the governing body of a municipality or county, if either of these finds that an emergency exists. Authority to declare a state of emergency under this section may also be delegated by ordinance to the mayor of a municipality or to the chair of the board of county commissioners of a county.

(b) Emergency Area. - The emergency area shall be determined in accordance with the following:

(1) Unless another subdivision of this subsection is applicable, the emergency area shall not exceed the area over which the municipality or county has jurisdiction to enact general police-power ordinances. The governing body declaring the state of emergency may declare that the emergency area includes part or all of the governing body's jurisdiction. Unless the governing body declaring the state of emergency provides otherwise, the emergency area includes this entire jurisdiction, subject to the limitations contained in the other subdivisions in this subsection.

(2) The emergency area of a state of emergency declared by a county shall not include any area within the corporate limits of any municipality, or within any area of the county over which a municipality has jurisdiction to enact general police-power ordinances, unless the municipality's governing body or mayor consents to or requests the state of emergency's application. Such an extension may be with respect to one or more of the prohibitions and restrictions imposed in that county pursuant to the authority granted in G.S. 166A-19.31 and need not be with respect to all prohibitions and restrictions authorized by that section.

(3) The board of commissioners or chair of the board of commissioners of any county who has been requested to do so by a mayor may by declaration extend the emergency area of a state of emergency declared by a municipality to any area within the county in which the board or chair determines it to be necessary to assist in the controlling of the emergency within the municipality. The extension may be with respect to one or more of the prohibitions and restrictions imposed in that mayor's municipality pursuant to the authority granted in G.S. 166A-19.31 and need not be with respect to all prohibitions and restrictions authorized by that section. Extension of the emergency area pursuant to this subdivision shall be subject to the following additional limitations:

a. The extension of the emergency area shall not include any area within the corporate limits of a municipality, or within any area of the county over which a municipality has jurisdiction to enact general police-power ordinances, unless the mayor or governing body of that other municipality consents to its application.

b. A chair of a board of county commissioners extending the emergency area under the authority of this subdivision shall take reasonable steps to give notice of its terms to those likely to be affected.

c. The chair of the board of commissioners shall declare the termination of any prohibitions and restrictions extended pursuant to this subdivision upon the earlier of the following:

1. The chair's determination that they are no longer necessary.

2. The determination of the board of county commissioners that they are no longer necessary.

3. The termination of the prohibitions and restrictions within the municipality.

d. The powers authorized under this subdivision may be exercised whether or not the county has enacted ordinances under the authority of G.S. 166A-19.31. Exercise of this authority shall not preclude the imposition of prohibitions and restrictions under any ordinances enacted by the county under the authority of G.S. 166A-19.31.

(c) Expiration of States of Emergency. - Unless an ordinance adopted pursuant to G.S. 166A-19.31 provides otherwise, a state of emergency declared pursuant to this section shall expire when it is terminated by the official or governing body that declared it.

(d) Effect of Declaration. - The declaration of a state of emergency pursuant to this section shall activate the local ordinances authorized in G.S. 166A-19.31 and any and all applicable local plans, mutual assistance compacts, and agreements and shall also authorize the furnishing of assistance thereunder. (Former G.S. 14-288.13: 1969, c. 869, s. 1; 1993, c. 539, s. 195; 1994, Ex. Sess., c. 24, s. 14(c). Former G.S. 14-288.14: 1969, c. 869, s. 1; 1993, c. 539, s. 196; 1994, Ex. Sess., c. 14, s. 7; c. 24, s. 14(c). Former G.S. 166A-8: 1951, c. 1016, s. 6; 1953, c. 1099, s. 4; 1957, c. 950, s. 2; 1959, c. 337, s. 5; 1973, c. 620, s. 9; 1975, c. 734, ss. 12, 14, 16; 1977, c. 848, s. 2; 2012-12, s. 1(b).)

§ 166A-19.23. Excessive pricing prohibitions.

A declaration issued pursuant to this Article shall trigger the prohibitions against excessive pricing during states of disaster, states of emergency, or abnormal market disruptions pursuant to G.S. 75-37 and G.S. 75-38. (2012-12, s. 1(b).)

§ 166A-19.24: Reserved for future codification purposes.

§ 166A-19.25: Reserved for future codification purposes.

§ 166A-19.26: Reserved for future codification purposes.

§ 166A-19.27: Reserved for future codification purposes.

§ 166A-19.28: Reserved for future codification purposes.

§ 166A-19.29: Reserved for future codification purposes.

Part 5. Additional Powers During States of Emergency.

§ 166A-19.30. Additional powers of the Governor during state of emergency.

(a) In addition to any other powers conferred upon the Governor by law, during a gubernatorially or legislatively declared state of emergency, the Governor shall have the following powers:

(1) To utilize all available State resources as reasonably necessary to cope with an emergency, including the transfer and direction of personnel or functions of State agencies or units thereof for the purpose of performing or facilitating emergency services.

(2) To take such action and give such directions to State and local law enforcement officers and agencies as may be reasonable and necessary for the purpose of securing compliance with the provisions of this Article and with the orders, rules, and regulations made pursuant thereto.

(3) To take steps to assure that measures, including the installation of public utilities, are taken when necessary to qualify for temporary housing assistance from the federal government when that assistance is required to protect the public health, welfare, and safety.

(4) Subject to the provisions of the State Constitution to relieve any public official having administrative responsibilities under this Article of such responsibilities for willful failure to obey an order, rule, or regulation adopted pursuant to this Article.

(b) During a gubernatorially or legislatively declared state of emergency, with the concurrence of the Council of State, the Governor has the following powers:

(1) To direct and compel the evacuation of all or part of the population from any stricken or threatened area within the State, to prescribe routes, modes of transportation, and destinations in connection with evacuation; and to control ingress and egress of an emergency area, the movement of persons within the area, and the occupancy of premises therein.

(2) To establish a system of economic controls over all resources, materials, and services to include food, clothing, shelter, fuel, rents, and wages, including the administration and enforcement of any rationing, price freezing, or similar federal order or regulation.

(3) To regulate and control the flow of vehicular and pedestrian traffic, the congregation of persons in public places or buildings, lights and noises of all

kinds, and the maintenance, extension, and operation of public utility and transportation services and facilities.

(4) To waive a provision of any regulation or ordinance of a State agency or a political subdivision which restricts the immediate relief of human suffering.

(5) To perform and exercise such other functions, powers, and duties as are necessary to promote and secure the safety and protection of the civilian population.

(6) To appoint or remove an executive head of any State agency or institution, the executive head of which is regularly selected by a State board or commission.

a. Such an acting executive head will serve during the following:

1. The physical or mental incapacity of the regular office holder, as determined by the Governor after such inquiry as the Governor deems appropriate.

2. The continued absence of the regular holder of the office.

3. A vacancy in the office pending selection of a new executive head.

b. An acting executive head of a State agency or institution appointed in accordance with this subdivision may perform any act and exercise any power which a regularly selected holder of such office could lawfully perform and exercise.

c. All powers granted to an acting executive head of a State agency or institution under this section shall expire immediately:

1. Upon the termination of the incapacity as determined by the Governor of the officer in whose stead the Governor acts;

2. Upon the return of the officer in whose stead the Governor acts; or

3. Upon the selection and qualification of a person to serve for the unexpired term, or the selection of an acting executive head of the agency or institution by the board or commission authorized to make such selection, and the person's qualification.

(7) To procure, by purchase, condemnation, seizure, or by other means to construct, lease, transport, store, maintain, renovate, or distribute materials and facilities for emergency management without regard to the limitation of any existing law.

(c) In addition to any other powers conferred upon the Governor by law, during a gubernatorially or legislatively declared state of emergency, if the Governor determines that local control of the emergency is insufficient to assure adequate protection for lives and property because (i) needed control cannot be imposed locally because local authorities responsible for preservation of the public peace have not enacted appropriate ordinances or issued appropriate declarations as authorized by G.S. 166A-19.31; (ii) local authorities have not taken implementing steps under such ordinances or declarations, if enacted or declared, for effectual control of the emergency that has arisen; (iii) the area in which the emergency exists has spread across local jurisdictional boundaries, and the legal control measures of the jurisdictions are conflicting or uncoordinated to the extent that efforts to protect life and property are, or unquestionably will be, severely hampered; or (iv) the scale of the emergency is so great that it exceeds the capability of local authorities to cope with it, the Governor has the following powers:

(1) To impose by declaration prohibitions and restrictions in the emergency area. These prohibitions and restrictions may, in the Governor's discretion, as appropriate to deal with the emergency, impose any of the types of prohibitions and restrictions enumerated in G.S. 166A-19.31(b), and may amend or rescind any prohibitions and restrictions imposed by local authorities. Prohibitions and restrictions imposed pursuant to this subdivision shall take effect in accordance with the provisions of G.S. 166A-19.31(d) and shall expire upon the earliest occurrence of either of the following: (i) the prohibition or restriction is terminated by the Governor or (ii) the state of emergency is terminated.

(2) Give to all participating State and local agencies and officers such directions as may be necessary to assure coordination among them. These directions may include the designation of the officer or agency responsible for directing and controlling the participation of all public agencies and officers in the emergency. The Governor may make this designation in any manner which, in the Governor's discretion, seems most likely to be effective. Any law enforcement officer participating in the control of a state of emergency in which the Governor is exercising control under this section shall have the same power and authority as a sheriff throughout the territory to which the law enforcement officer is assigned.

(d)   Violation. - Any person who violates any provision of a declaration or executive order issued pursuant to this section shall be guilty of a Class 2 misdemeanor in accordance with G.S. 14-288.20A. (Former G.S. 14-288.15: 1969, c. 869, s. 1; 1993, c. 539, s. 197; 1994, Ex. Sess., c. 24, s. 14(c). Former G.S. 166A-6: 1951, c. 1016, s. 4; 1955, c. 387, s. 4; 1959, c. 284, s. 2; c. 337, s. 4; 1975, c. 734, ss. 11, 14; 1977, c. 848, s. 2; 1979, 2nd Sess., c. 1310, s. 2; 1993, c. 321, s. 181(a); 1995, c. 509, s. 125; 2001-214, s. 3; 2011-145, s. 19.1(g); 2011-183, s. 127(c); 2012-90, s. 1; 2012-12, s. 1(b).)

§ 166A-19.31. Power of municipalities and counties to enact ordinances to deal with states of emergency.

(a)   Authority to Enact Prohibitions and Restrictions. - The governing body of any municipality or county may enact ordinances designed to permit the imposition of prohibitions and restrictions within the emergency area during a state of emergency declared pursuant to G.S. 166A-19.22. Authority to impose by declaration prohibitions and restrictions under this section, and to impose those prohibitions and restrictions at a particular time as appropriate, may be delegated by ordinance to the mayor of a municipality or to the chair of the board of county commissioners of a county.

(b)   Type of Prohibitions and Restrictions Authorized. - The ordinances authorized by this section may permit prohibitions and restrictions:

(1)   Of movements of people in public places, including imposing a curfew; directing and compelling the voluntary or mandatory evacuation of all or part of the population from any stricken or threatened area within the governing body's jurisdiction; prescribing routes, modes of transportation, and destinations in connection with evacuation; and controlling ingress and egress of an emergency area, and the movement of persons within the area.

(2)   Of the operation of offices, business establishments, and other places to or from which people may travel or at which they may congregate.

(3)   Upon the possession, transportation, sale, purchase, and consumption of alcoholic beverages.

(4)   Upon the possession, transportation, sale, purchase, storage, and use of gasoline, and dangerous weapons and substances, except that this subdivision does not authorize prohibitions or restrictions on lawfully possessed

firearms or ammunition. As used in this subdivision, the term "dangerous weapons and substances" has the same meaning as it does under G.S. 14-288.1. As used in this subdivision, the term "firearm" has the same meaning as it does under G.S. 14-409.39(2).

(5)   Upon other activities or conditions the control of which may be reasonably necessary to maintain order and protect lives or property during the state of emergency.

The ordinances authorized by this section need not require or provide for the imposition of all of the types of prohibitions or restrictions, or any particular prohibition or restriction, authorized by this section during an emergency but may instead authorize the official or officials who impose those prohibitions or restrictions to determine and impose the prohibitions or restrictions deemed necessary or suitable to a particular state of emergency.

(c)   When Ordinances Take Effect. - Notwithstanding any other provision of law, whether general or special, relating to the promulgation or publication of ordinances by any municipality or county, upon the declaration of a state of emergency by the mayor or chair of the board of county commissioners within the municipality or the county, any ordinance enacted under the authority of this section shall take effect immediately unless the ordinance sets a later time. If the effect of this section is to cause an ordinance to go into effect sooner than it otherwise could under the law applicable to the municipality or county, the mayor or chair of the board of county commissioners, as the case may be, shall take steps to cause reports of the substance of the ordinance to be disseminated in a fashion that its substance will likely be communicated to the public in general, or to those who may be particularly affected by the ordinance if it does not affect the public generally. As soon as practicable thereafter, appropriate distribution or publication of the full text of any such ordinance shall be made.

(d)   When Prohibitions and Restrictions Take Effect. - All prohibitions and restrictions imposed by declaration pursuant to ordinances adopted under this section shall take effect in the emergency area immediately upon publication of the declaration unless the declaration sets a later time. For the purpose of requiring compliance, publication may consist of reports of the substance of the prohibitions and restrictions in the mass communications media serving the emergency area or other effective methods of disseminating the necessary information quickly. As soon as practicable, however, appropriate distribution of the full text of any declaration shall be made. This subsection shall not be governed by the provisions of G.S. 1-597.

(e)   Expiration of Prohibitions and Restrictions. - Prohibitions and restrictions imposed pursuant to this section shall expire upon the earliest occurrence of any of the following:

(1)   The prohibition or restriction is terminated by the official or entity that imposed the prohibition or restriction.

(2)   The state of emergency terminates.

(f)   Intent to Supplement Other Authority. - This section is intended to supplement and confirm the powers conferred by G.S. 153A-121(a), G.S. 160A-174(a), and all other general and local laws authorizing municipalities and counties to enact ordinances for the protection of the public health and safety in times of riot or other grave civil disturbance or emergency.

(g)   Previously Enacted Ordinances Remain in Effect. - Any ordinance of a type authorized by this section promulgated prior to October 1, 2012, if otherwise valid, continue in full force and effect without reenactment.

(h)   Violation. - Any person who violates any provision of an ordinance or a declaration enacted or declared pursuant to this section shall be guilty of a Class 2 misdemeanor in accordance with G.S. 14-288.20A. (Former G.S. 14-288.12: 1969, c. 869, s. 1; 1981, c. 412, s. 4(4); c. 747, s. 66; 1989, c. 770, s. 2; 1993, c. 539, s. 194; 1994, Ex. Sess., c. 24, s. 14(c); 2009-146, s. 1. Former G.S. 14-288.13: 1969, c. 869, s. 1; 1993, c. 539, s. 195; 1994, Ex. Sess., c. 24, s. 14(c). Former G.S. 14-288.16: 1969, c. 869, s. 1. Former G.S. 14-288.17: 1969, c. 869, s. 1. 2012-12, s. 1(b).)

§ 166A-19.32: Reserved for future codification purposes.

§ 166A-19.33: Reserved for future codification purposes.

§ 166A-19.34: Reserved for future codification purposes.

§ 166A-19.35: Reserved for future codification purposes.

§ 166A-19.36: Reserved for future codification purposes.

§ 166A-19.37: Reserved for future codification purposes.

§ 166A-19.38: Reserved for future codification purposes.

§ 166A-19.39: Reserved for future codification purposes.

Part 6. Funding of Emergency Preparedness and Response.

§ 166A-19.40. Use of contingency and emergency funds.

(a) Use of Funds for Relief and Assistance. - The Governor may use contingency and emergency funds as necessary and appropriate to provide relief and assistance from the effects of an emergency and may reallocate such other funds as may reasonably be available within the appropriations of the various departments when the severity and magnitude of the emergency so requires and the contingency and emergency funds are insufficient or inappropriate.

(b) Use of Funds for National Guard Training. - In preparation for a state of emergency, with the concurrence of the Council of State, the Governor may use contingency and emergency funds as necessary and appropriate for National Guard training in preparation for emergencies. (Former G.S. 166A-5: 1951, c. 1016, ss. 3, 9; 1953, c. 1099, s. 3; 1955, c. 387, ss. 2, 3, 5; 1957, c. 950, s. 5; 1975, c. 734, ss. 9, 10, 14, 16; 1977, c. 848, s. 2; 1979, 2nd Sess., c. 1310, s. 2; 1995, c. 509, s. 124; 2001-214, s. 2; 2002-179, s. 12; 2009-192, s. 1; 2009-193, s. 3; 2009-196, s. 1; 2009-225, s. 1; 2011-145, s. 19.1(g). Former G.S. 166A-6: 1951, c. 1016, s. 4; 1955, c. 387, s. 4; 1959, c. 284, s. 2; c. 337, s. 4; 1975, c. 734, ss. 11, 14; 1977, c. 848, s. 2; 1979, 2nd Sess., c. 1310, s. 2; 1993, c. 321, s. 181(a); 1995, c. 509, s. 125; 2001-214, s. 3; 2011-145, s. 19.1(g); 2011-183, s. 127(c); 2012-12, s. 1(b).)

§ 166A-19.41. State emergency assistance funds.

(a) Governor May Make Funds Available for Emergency Assistance. - In the event of a gubernatorially or legislatively declared state of emergency, the Governor may make State funds available for emergency assistance as authorized by this section. Any State funds made available by the Governor for emergency assistance may be administered through State emergency assistance programs which may be established by the Governor upon the declaration of a state of emergency. It is the intent of the General Assembly in authorizing the Governor to make State funds available for emergency assistance and in authorizing the Governor to establish State emergency assistance programs to provide State assistance for recovery from those emergencies for which federal assistance under the Stafford Act is either not available or does not adequately meet the needs of the citizens of the State in the emergency area.

(b) Emergency Assistance in a Type I Disaster. - In the event that a Type I disaster is declared, the Governor may make State funds available for emergency assistance in the emergency area in the form of individual assistance and public assistance as provided in this subsection.

(1) Individual assistance. - State emergency assistance in the form of grants to individuals and families may be made available when damage meets or exceeds the criteria set out in 13 C.F.R. Part 123 for the Small Business Administration Disaster Loan Program. Individual assistance grants shall include benefits comparable to those provided by the Stafford Act and may be provided for the following:

a. Provision of temporary housing and rental assistance.

b. Repair or replacement of dwellings. Grants for repair or replacement of housing may include amounts necessary to locate the individual or family in safe, decent, and sanitary housing.

c. Replacement of personal property (including clothing, tools, and equipment).

d. Repair or replacement of privately owned vehicles.

e. Medical or dental expenses.

f. Funeral or burial expenses resulting from the emergency.

g. Funding for the cost of the first year's flood insurance premium to meet the requirements of the National Flood Insurance Act of 1968, as amended, 42 U.S.C. § 4001, et seq.

(2) Public assistance. - State emergency assistance in the form of public assistance grants may be made available to eligible entities located within the emergency area on the following terms and conditions:

a. Eligible entities shall meet the following qualifications:

1. The eligible entity suffers a minimum of ten thousand dollars ($10,000) in uninsurable losses.

2. The eligible entity suffers uninsurable losses in an amount equal to or exceeding one percent (1%) of the annual operating budget.

3. For a state of emergency declared pursuant to G.S. 166A-19.20(a) after the deadline established by the Federal Emergency Management Agency pursuant to the Disaster Mitigation Act of 2002, P.L. 106-390, the eligible entity shall have a hazard mitigation plan approved pursuant to the Stafford Act.

4. For a state of emergency declared pursuant to G.S. 166A-19.20(a), after August 1, 2002, the eligible entity shall be participating in the National Flood Insurance Program in order to receive public assistance for flooding damage.

b. Eligible entities shall be required to provide non-State matching funds equal to twenty-five percent (25%) of the eligible costs of the public assistance grant.

c. An eligible entity that receives a public assistance grant pursuant to this subsection may use the grant for the following purposes only:

1. Debris clearance.

2. Emergency protective measures.

3. Roads and bridges.

4. Crisis counseling.

5. Assistance with public transportation needs.

(c) Emergency Assistance in a Type II Disaster. - If a Type II disaster is declared, the Governor may make State funds available for emergency assistance in the emergency area in the form of the following types of grants:

(1)   State Acquisition and Relocation Funds.

(2)   Supplemental repair and replacement housing grants available to individuals or families in an amount necessary to locate the individual or family in safe, decent, and sanitary housing, not to exceed twenty-five thousand dollars ($25,000) per family.

(d)   Emergency Assistance in a Type III Disaster. - If a Type III disaster is declared, the Governor may make State funds available for emergency assistance in the emergency area in the form of the following types of grants:

(1)   State Acquisition and Relocation Funds.

(2)   Supplemental repair and replacement housing grants available to individuals or families in an amount necessary to locate the individual or family in safe, decent, and sanitary housing, not to exceed twenty-five thousand dollars ($25,000) per family.

(3)   Any programs authorized by the General Assembly. (2001-214, s. 4; 2001-487, s. 98; 2002-24, s. 1; 2002-159, s. 57.5; 2006-66, s. 6.5(a); 2012-12, s. 1(b).)

§ 166A-19.42. State Emergency Response Account.

(a)   Account Established. - There is established a State Emergency Response Account as a reserve in the General Fund. Any funds appropriated to the Account shall remain available for expenditure as provided by this section, unless directed otherwise by the General Assembly.

(b)   Use of Funds. - The Governor may spend funds from the Account for the following purposes:

(1)   To cover the start-up costs of State Emergency Response Team operations for an emergency that poses an imminent threat of a Type I, Type II, or Type III disaster.

(2)   To cover the cost of first responders to a Type I, Type II, or Type III disaster and any related supplies and equipment needed by first responders that are not provided for under subdivision (1) of this subsection.

All other types of emergency assistance authorized by this Part shall continue to be financed by the funds made available under G.S. 166A-19.41.

(c) Reporting Requirement. - The Governor shall report to the Joint Legislative Commission on Governmental Operations and to the Chairs of the Appropriations Committees of the Senate and House of Representatives on any expenditures from the State Emergency Response Account no later than 30 days after making the expenditure. The report shall include a description of the emergency and type of action taken. (2006-66, s. 6.5(b); 2012-12, s. 1(b).)

§ 166A-19.43: Reserved for future codification purposes.

§ 166A-19.44: Reserved for future codification purposes.

§ 166A-19.45: Reserved for future codification purposes.

§ 166A-19.46: Reserved for future codification purposes.

§ 166A-19.47: Reserved for future codification purposes.

§ 166A-19.48: Reserved for future codification purposes.

§ 166A-19.49: Reserved for future codification purposes.

§ 166A-19.50: Reserved for future codification purposes.

§ 166A-19.51: Reserved for future codification purposes.

§ 166A-19.52: Reserved for future codification purposes.

§ 166A-19.53: Reserved for future codification purposes.

§ 166A-19.54: Reserved for future codification purposes.

§ 166A-19.55: Reserved for future codification purposes.

§ 166A-19.56: Reserved for future codification purposes.

§ 166A-19.57: Reserved for future codification purposes.

§ 166A-19.58: Reserved for future codification purposes.

§ 166A-19.59: Reserved for future codification purposes.

Part 7. Immunity and Liability.

§ 166A-19.60. Immunity and exemption.

(a)   Generally. - All functions hereunder and all other activities relating to emergency management as provided for in this Chapter or elsewhere in the General Statutes are hereby declared to be governmental functions. Neither the State nor any political subdivision thereof, nor, except in cases of willful misconduct, gross negligence, or bad faith, any emergency management worker, firm, partnership, association, or corporation complying with or reasonably attempting to comply with this Article or any order, rule, or regulation promulgated pursuant to the provisions of this Article or pursuant to any ordinance relating to any emergency management measures enacted by any political subdivision of the State, shall be liable for the death of or injury to persons, or for damage to property as a result of any such activity.

(b)   Immunity. - The immunity provided to firms, partnerships, associations, or corporations, under subsection (a) of this section, is subject to all of the following conditions:

(1)   The immunity applies only when the firm, partnership, association, or corporation is acting without compensation or with compensation limited to no more than actual expenses and one of the following applies:

a.   Emergency management services are provided at any place in this State during a state of emergency declared by the Governor or General Assembly pursuant to this Article, and the services are provided under the direction and control of the Secretary pursuant to G.S. 166A-19.10, 166A-19.11, 166A-19.12, 166A-19.20, 166A-19.30, and 143B-602, or the Governor.

b.   Emergency management services are provided during a state of emergency declared pursuant to G.S. 166A-19.22, and the services are provided under the direction and control of the governing body of a municipality or county under G.S. 166A-19.31, or the chair of a board of county commissioners under G.S. 166A-19.22(b)(3).

c. The firm, partnership, association, or corporation is engaged in planning, preparation, training, or exercises with the Division, the Division of Public Health, or the governing body of each county or municipality under G.S. 166A-19.15 related to the performance of emergency management services or measures.

(2) The immunity shall not apply to any firm, partnership, association, or corporation, or to any employee or agent thereof, whose act or omission caused in whole or in part the actual or imminent emergency or whose act or omission necessitated emergency management measures.

(3) To the extent that any firm, partnership, association, or corporation has liability insurance, that firm, partnership, association, or corporation shall be deemed to have waived the immunity to the extent of the indemnification by insurance for its negligence. An insurer shall not under a contract of insurance exclude from liability coverage the acts or omissions of a firm, partnership, association, or corporation for which the firm, partnership, association, or corporation would only be liable to the extent indemnified by insurance as provided by this subdivision.

(c) No Effect on Benefits. - The rights of any person to receive benefits to which the person would otherwise be entitled under this Article or under the Workers' Compensation Law or under any pension law and the right of any such person to receive any benefits or compensation under any act of Congress shall not be affected by performance of emergency management functions.

(d) License Requirements Suspended. - Any requirement for a license to practice any professional, mechanical, or other skill shall not apply to any authorized emergency management worker who shall, in the course of performing the worker's duties as such, practice such professional, mechanical, or other skill during a state of emergency.

(e) Definition of Emergency Management Worker. - As used in this section, the term "emergency management worker" shall include any full or part-time paid, volunteer, or auxiliary employee of this State or other states, territories, possessions, or the District of Columbia, of the federal government or any neighboring country or of any political subdivision thereof, or of any agency or organization performing emergency management services at any place in this

State, subject to the order or control of or pursuant to a request of the State government or any political subdivision thereof. The term "emergency management worker" under this section shall also include any health care worker performing health care services as a member of a hospital-based or county-based State Medical Assistance Team designated by the North Carolina Office of Emergency Medical Services and any person performing emergency health care services under G.S. 90-12.2.

(f) Powers of Individuals Operating Pursuant to Mutual Aid Agreements. - Any emergency management worker, as defined in this section, performing emergency management services at any place in this State pursuant to agreements, compacts, or arrangements for mutual aid and assistance to which the State or a political subdivision thereof is a party, shall possess the same powers, duties, immunities, and privileges the person would ordinarily possess if performing duties in the State, or political subdivision thereof, in which normally employed or rendering services. (1957, c. 950, s. 4; 1975, c. 734, s. 14; 1977, c. 848, s. 2; 1979, c. 714, s. 2; 1979, 2nd Sess., c. 1310, s. 2; 1995, c. 509, ss. 130, 131; 2002-179, s. 20(b); 2006-81, s. 1; 2008-200, s. 1; 2009-146, s. 2; 2011-145, s. 19.1(g), (hhh); 2012-12, s. 1(b).)

§ 166A-19.61. No private liability.

Any person, firm, or corporation, together with any successors in interest, if any, owning or controlling real or personal property who, voluntarily or involuntarily, knowingly or unknowingly, with or without compensation, grants a license or privilege or otherwise permits or allows the designation or use of the whole or any part or parts of such real or personal property for the purpose of activities or functions relating to emergency management as provided for in this Chapter or elsewhere in the General Statutes shall not be civilly liable for the death of or injury to any person or the loss of or damage to the property of any persons where such death, injury, loss, or damage resulted from, through, or because of the use of the said real or personal property for any of the above purposes, provided that the use of said property is subject to the order or control of or pursuant to a request of the State government or any political subdivision thereof. (1957, c. 950, s. 3; 1977, c. 848, s. 2; 2012-12, s. 1(b); 2012-90, s. 9.)

§ 166A-19.62. Civil liability of persons who willfully ignore a warning in an emergency.

In an emergency, a person who willfully ignores a warning regarding personal safety issued by a federal, State, or local law enforcement agency, emergency management agency, or other governmental agency responsible for emergency management under this Article is civilly liable for the cost of a rescue effort to any governmental agency or nonprofit agency cooperating with a governmental agency conducting a rescue on the endangered person's behalf if all of the following are true:

(1) The person ignores the warning and (i) engages in an activity or course of action that a reasonable person would not pursue or (ii) fails to take a course of action that a reasonable person would pursue.

(2) As a result of ignoring the warning, the person places himself or herself or another in danger.

(3) A governmental rescue effort is undertaken on the endangered person's behalf. (1997-232, s. 1; 2012-12, s. 1(b).)

§ 166A-19.63: Reserved for future codification purposes.

§ 166A-19.64: Reserved for future codification purposes.

§ 166A-19.65: Reserved for future codification purposes.

§ 166A-19.66: Reserved for future codification purposes.

§ 166A-19.67: Reserved for future codification purposes.

§ 166A-19.68: Reserved for future codification purposes.

§ 166A-19.69: Reserved for future codification purposes.

Part 8. Miscellaneous Provisions.

§ 166A-19.70. Ensuring availability of emergency supplies and utility services; protection of livestock, poultry, and agricultural crops.

(a) Executive Order. - In addition to any other powers conferred on the Governor by law, whenever a curfew has been imposed, the Governor may declare by executive order that the health, safety, or economic well-being of persons or property in this State require that persons transporting essentials in commerce to the curfew area, or assisting in ensuring their availability, and persons assisting in restoring utility services, be allowed to enter or remain in areas from which they would otherwise be excluded for the limited purpose of delivering the essentials, assisting in ensuring their availability, or assisting in restoring utility services.

(b) Maximum Hours of Service Waiver. - As part of an executive order issued pursuant to subsection (a) of this section, or independently of such an order, the Governor may declare by executive order that the health, safety, or economic well-being of persons or property in this State require that the maximum hours of service prescribed by the Department of Public Safety pursuant to G.S. 20-381 and similar rules be waived for persons transporting essentials or assisting in the restoration of utility services.

(c) Certification System. - The Secretary shall develop a system pursuant to which a person who transports essentials in commerce, or assists in ensuring their availability, and persons who assist in the restoring of utility services can be certified as such. The certification system shall allow for both preemergency declaration and postemergency declaration certification and may include an annually renewable precertification. The Secretary shall only allow those who routinely transport or distribute essentials or assist in the restoring of utility services to be certified. A certification of the employer shall constitute a certification of the employer's employees. The Secretary shall create an easily recognizable indicium of certification in order to assist local officials' efforts to determine which persons have received certification by the system established under this subsection.

(d) Presence in Curfew Area Permitted. - Notwithstanding the existence of any curfew, a person who is certified pursuant to the system established under subsection (c) of this section shall be allowed to enter or remain in the curfew area for the limited purpose of delivering or assisting in the distribution of essentials or assisting in the restoration of utility services and shall be allowed to provide service that exceeds otherwise applicable hours of service maximums, to the extent authorized by an executive order executed pursuant to subsection (a) of this section. Nothing in this section prohibits law enforcement or other local officials from specifying the permissible route of ingress or egress for persons with certifications.

(e) Abnormal Market Disruptions with Respect to Petroleum. - If the Governor declares the existence of an abnormal market disruption with respect to petroleum pursuant to G.S. 75-38(f), the Governor shall contemporaneously seek all applicable waivers under the federal Clean Air Act, 42 U.S.C. § 7401, et seq., and any other applicable federal law to facilitate the transportation of fuel within this State in order to address or prevent a fuel supply emergency in this State. Waiver requests shall be directed to the appropriate federal agencies and shall seek waivers of the following:

(1) The Reformulated Gasoline requirements throughout the State.

(2) The Federal and State Implementation Plan summertime gasoline requirements (low RVP) throughout the State.

(3) Any other waiver that will, if obtained, facilitate the transportation of fuel within this State.

(f) Definitions. - The following definitions apply in this section:

(1) Curfew. - Any restriction on ingress and egress to the emergency area of a state of emergency or any restriction on the movement of persons within such an area.

(2) Curfew area. - The area that is subject to a curfew.

(3) Essentials. - Any goods that are consumed or used as a direct result of an emergency or which are consumed or used to preserve, protect, or sustain life, health, safety, or economic well-being of persons or their property. The Secretary shall determine what goods constitute essentials for purposes of this section.

(g) Upon the recommendation of the Commissioner of Agriculture it shall be lawful for the Governor, by an executive order issued pursuant to G.S. 166A-19.20 or independently of such an order, to direct the Department of Public Safety to temporarily suspend weighing, pursuant to G.S. 20-118.1, those vehicles used to transport livestock, poultry, or crops from designated counties in an emergency area as defined in G.S. 166A-19.3(7), or counties designated by the Governor in an executive order issued independently of an order pursuant to G.S. 166A-19.20, if there exists an imminent threat of severe economic loss of livestock or poultry or widespread or severe damage to crops ready to be harvested. The Department of Public Safety shall develop procedures to carry out the provisions of this subsection. This subsection shall not be construed to permit the gross weight of any vehicle or combination in excess of the safe load carrying capacity established by the Department of Transportation on any bridge pursuant to G.S. 136-72, or to permit the operation of a vehicle when a law enforcement officer has probable cause to believe the vehicle is creating an imminent hazard to public safety. A suspension authorized pursuant to the provisions of this subsection shall end when the Governor determines the threat of widespread or severe loss or damage in the designated counties has passed. (2001-214, s. 4; 2001-487, s. 98; 2002-24, s. 1; 2002-159, s. 57.5; 2006-66, s. 6.5(a); 2012-12, s. 1(b); 2013-230, s. 1.)

§ 166A-19.71. Accept services, gifts, grants, and loans.

Whenever the federal government or any agency or officer thereof or of any person, firm, or corporation shall offer to the State, or through the State to any political subdivision thereof, services, equipment, supplies, materials, or funds by way of gift, grant, or loan, for emergency management purposes, the State acting through the Governor, or such political subdivision, acting with the consent of the Governor and through its governing body, may accept such offer. Upon such acceptance the Governor of the State or governing body of such political subdivision may authorize any officer of the State or of the political subdivision, as the case may be, to receive such services, equipment, supplies, materials, or funds on behalf of the State or of such political subdivision, and subject to the terms of the offer and the rules and regulations, if any, of the agency making the offer. (1951, c. 1016, s. 8; 1973, c. 803, s. 45; 1975, c. 19, s. 72; c. 734, ss. 13, 14; 1977, c. 848, s. 2; 1979, 2nd Sess., c. 1310, s. 2; 2012-12, s. 1(b).)

§ 166A-19.72. Establishment of mutual aid agreements.

(a) Governor Authorized to Enter Agreements with Other States and Federal Government. - The Governor may establish mutual aid agreements with other states and with the federal government provided that any special agreements so negotiated are within the Governor's authority.

(b) Governor Authorized to Enter Agreements with Political Subdivisions. - The Governor may establish mutual aid agreements with political subdivisions in the State with the concurrence of the subdivision's governing body.

(c) Political Subdivisions Authorized to Enter Agreements with Other Political Subdivisions. - The chief executive of each political subdivision, with the concurrence of the subdivision's governing body, may develop mutual aid agreements for reciprocal emergency management aid and assistance. Such agreements shall be consistent with the State emergency management program and plans.

(d) Political Subdivisions Authorized to Enter Agreements with Political Subdivisions in Other States. - The chief executive officer of each political subdivision, with the concurrence of the governing body and subject to the approval of the Governor, may enter into mutual aid agreements with local chief executive officers in other states for reciprocal emergency management aid and assistance. These agreements shall be consistent with the State emergency management program and plans.

(e) Terms of Agreements. - Mutual aid agreements may include, but are not limited to, the furnishing or exchange of such supplies, equipment, facilities, personnel, and services as may be needed; the reimbursement of costs and expenses for equipment, supplies, personnel, and similar items; and on such terms and conditions as deemed necessary. (1951, c. 1016, s. 7; 1975, c. 734, ss. 14, 16; 1977, c. 848, s. 2; 1979, 2nd Sess., c. 1310, s. 2; 2009-194, s. 1; 2012-12, s. 1(b).)

§ 166A-19.73. Compensation.

(a) Extent of Compensation. - Compensation for services or for the taking or use of property shall be only to the extent that legal obligations of individual citizens are exceeded in a particular case and then only to the extent that the claimant has not been deemed to have volunteered his services or property without compensation.

(b) Limitation; Basis of Compensation. - Compensation for property shall be only if the property was commandeered, seized, taken, condemned, or otherwise used in coping with an emergency and this action was ordered by the Governor. The State shall make compensation for the property so seized, taken, or condemned on the following basis:

(1) In case property is taken for temporary use, the Governor, within 30 days of the taking, shall fix the amount of compensation to be paid for such damage or failure to return. Whenever the Governor shall deem it advisable for

the State to take title to property taken under this section, the Governor shall forthwith cause the owner of such property to be notified thereof in writing by registered mail, postage prepaid, or by the best means available, and forthwith cause to be filed a copy of said notice with the Secretary of State.

(2) If the person entitled to receive the amounts so determined by the Governor as just compensation is unwilling to accept the same as full and complete compensation for such property or the use thereof, the person shall be paid seventy-five percent (75%) of such amount and shall be entitled to recover from the State of North Carolina in an action brought in the superior court in the county of residence of claimant, or in Wake County, in the same manner as other condemnation claims are brought, within three years after the date of the Governor's award. (1977, c. 848, s. 2; 2012-12, s. 1(b).)

§ 166A-19.74. Nondiscrimination in emergency management.

State and local governmental bodies and other organizations and personnel who carry out emergency management functions under the provisions of this Article are required to do so in an equitable and impartial manner. Such State and local governmental bodies, organizations, and personnel shall not discriminate on the grounds of race, color, religion, nationality, sex, age, or economic status in the distribution of supplies, the processing of applications, and other relief and assistance activities. (1975, c. 734, s. 3; 1977, c. 848, s. 2; 1979, 2nd Sess., c. 1310, s. 2; 1995, c. 509, s. 128; 2012-12, s. 1(b).)

§ 166A-19.75. Emergency management personnel.

(a) Limitation. - No person shall be employed or associated in any capacity in any emergency management agency established under this Article if that person does or has done any of the following:

(1) Advocates or has advocated a change by force or violence in the constitutional form of the Government of the United States or in this State.

(2) Advocates or has advocated the overthrow of any government in the United States by force or violence.

(3) Has been convicted of any subversive act against the United States.

(4) Is under indictment or information charging any subversive act against the United States.

(5) Has ever been a member of the Communist Party.

(b) Oath. - Each person who is appointed to serve in any emergency management agency shall, before entering upon the person's duties, take a written oath before a person authorized to administer oaths in this State, which oath shall be substantially as follows:

"I, _____, do solemnly swear (or affirm) that I will support and defend the Constitution of the United States and the Constitution of the State of North Carolina, against all enemies, foreign and domestic; and that I will bear true faith and allegiance to the same; that I take this obligation freely, without any mental reservation or purpose of evasion; and that I will well and faithfully discharge the duties upon which I am about to enter. And I do further swear (or affirm) that I do not advocate, nor am I, nor have I ever knowingly been, a member of any political party or organization that advocates the overthrow of the Government of the United States or of this State by force or violence; and that during such time as I am a member of the State Emergency Management Agency I will not advocate nor become a member of any political party or organization that advocates the overthrow of the Government of the United States or of this State by force or violence, so help me God."

(c) No Violation of Dual Office Holding Prohibition. - No position created by or pursuant to this Article shall be deemed an office within the meaning of Section 9 of Article 6 of the North Carolina Constitution. (1951, c. 1016, s. 10; 1975, c. 734, ss. 14, 16; 1977, c. 848, s. 2; 1979, 2nd Sess., c. 1310, s. 2; 1995, c. 509, s. 129; 2012-12, s. 1(b).)

§ 166A-19.76. Leave options for voluntary firefighters, rescue squad workers, and emergency medical service personnel called into service.

(a) Leave Without Pay. - A member of a volunteer fire department, rescue squad, or emergency medical services agency called into service of the State after a declaration of a state of emergency by the Governor or by the General Assembly, or upon the activation of the State Emergency Response Team in response to an emergency, shall have the right to take leave without pay from his or her civilian employment. No member of a volunteer fire department, rescue squad, or emergency medical services agency shall be forced to use or exhaust his or her vacation or other accrued leave from his or her civilian employment for a period of active service. The choice of leave shall be solely within the discretion of the member.

(b) Request in Writing Required. - For the volunteer member to be entitled to take leave without pay pursuant to this section, his or her services shall be requested in writing by the Director of the Division or by the head of a local emergency management agency. The request shall be directed to the Chief of the member's volunteer fire department, rescue squad, or emergency medical services agency, and a copy shall be provided to the member's employer. This section shall not apply to those members whose services have been certified by their employer to the Director of the Division, or to the head of a local emergency management agency, as essential to the employer's own ongoing emergency relief activities.

(c) Definition of an Emergency Requiring Activation of the State Emergency Response Team. - For purposes of this section, an emergency requiring the activation of the State Emergency Response Team means an emergency at Activation Level 2 or greater according to the North Carolina State Emergency Operations Plan of November 2002. Activation Level 2 requires the State Emergency Operations Center to be fully activated with 24-hour staffing from all State Emergency Response Team members.

(d) Enforcement. - The Commissioner of Labor shall enforce the provisions of this section pursuant to Chapter 95 of the General Statutes. (2003-103, s. 1; 2012-12, s. 1(b).)

§ 166A-19.77. North Carolina Forest Service designated as emergency response agency.

The North Carolina Forest Service of the Department of Agriculture and Consumer Services is designated an emergency response agency of the State of North Carolina for purposes of the following:

(1) Supporting the North Carolina Forest Service in responding to all-risk incidents.

(2) Receipt of any applicable State or federal funding.

(3) Training of other State and local agencies in emergency management.

(4) Any other emergency response roles for which the North Carolina Forest Service has special training or qualifications. (2005-128, s. 1; 2011-145, ss. 13.25(ww), 19.1(g); 2012-12, s. 1(b); 2013-155, s. 24.)

§ 166A-19.78. Governor's power to order evacuation of public building.

When it is determined by the Governor that a great public crisis, disaster, riot, catastrophe, or any other similar public emergency exists, or the occurrence of any such condition is imminent, and, in the Governor's opinion it is necessary to evacuate any building owned or controlled by any department, agency, institution, school, college, board, division, commission, or subdivision of the State in order to maintain public order and safety or to afford adequate protection for lives or property, the Governor is hereby authorized to issue an order of evacuation directing all persons within the building to leave the building and its premises forthwith. The order shall be delivered to any law enforcement officer or officer of the National Guard, and such officer shall, by a suitable public address system, read the order to the occupants of the building and demand that the occupants forthwith evacuate said building within the time specified in the Governor's order. (1969, c. 1129; 1993, c. 539, s. 198; 1994, Ex. Sess., c. 24, s. 14(c); 2009-281, s. 1; 2012-12, s. 1(b).)

§ 166A-19.79. Severability.

If any provision of this Article or the application thereof to any person or circumstances is held invalid, the invalidity does not affect other provisions or applications of the Article which can be given effect without the invalid provision or application, and to this end the provisions of this Article are severable. (1977, c. 848, s. 2; 1995, c. 509, s. 132; 2012-12, s. 1(b).)

Article 2.

Hazardous Materials Emergency Response.

§ 166A-20. Title, purpose.

(a) This Article may be cited as the "North Carolina Hazardous Materials Emergency Response Act."

(b) The purpose of this Article is to establish a system of regional response to hazardous materials emergencies and terrorist incidents in the State to protect the health and safety of its citizens. (1993 (Reg. Sess., 1994), c. 769, s. 22.4(b); 2002-179, s. 21(a).)

§ 166A-21. Definitions.

As used in this Article:

(1) "Hazardous materials emergency response team" or "hazmat team" means an organized group of persons specially trained and equipped to respond to and control actual or potential leaks or spills of hazardous materials.

(2) "Hazardous material" means any material defined as a hazardous substance under 29 Code of Federal Regulations § 1910.120(a)(3).

(3) "Hazardous materials incident" or "hazardous materials emergency" means an uncontrolled release or threatened release of a hazardous substance requiring outside assistance by a local fire department or hazmat team to contain and control.

(4) "Regional response team" means a hazmat team under contract with the State to provide response to hazardous materials emergencies occurring outside the hazmat team's local jurisdiction at the direction of the Department of Public Safety, Division of Emergency Management.

(5) "Secretary" means the Secretary of the Department of Public Safety.

(6) "Technician-level entry capability" means the capacity of a hazmat team, in terms of training and equipment as specified in 29 Code of Federal Regulations § 1910.120, to respond to a hazardous materials incident requiring affirmative measures, such as patching, plugging, or other action necessary to stop and contain the release of a hazardous substance at its source.

(7) "Terrorist incident" means activities that occur within the territorial jurisdiction of the United States, involve acts dangerous to human life that are a violation of the criminal laws of the United States or of any state, and are intended to do one of the following:

a. Intimidate or coerce a civilian population.

b. Influence the policy of a government by intimidation or coercion.

c. Affect the conduct of a government by mass destruction, assassination, or kidnapping. (1993 (Reg. Sess., 1994), c. 769, s. 22.4(b); 1997-456, s. 27; 2002-179, s. 21(b); 2011-145, s. 19.1(g).)

§ 166A-22. Hazardous materials emergency response program.

(a) The Secretary shall adopt rules establishing a regional response program for hazardous materials emergencies and terrorist incidents, to be administered by the Division of Emergency Management. To the extent possible, the regional response program shall be coordinated with other emergency planning activities of the State. The regional response program shall include at least six hazmat teams located strategically across the State that are available to provide regional response to hazardous materials or terrorist incidents requiring technician-level entry capability and 24-hour dispatch and communications capability at the Division of Emergency Management Operations Center. The rules for the program shall include:

(1) Standards, including training, equipment, and personnel standards required to operate a regional response team with technician-level entry capability.

(2) Guidelines for the dispatch of a regional response team to a hazardous materials or terrorist incident.

(3) Guidelines for the on-site operations of a regional response team.

(4) Standards for administration of a regional response team, including procedures for reimbursement of response costs.

(5) Refresher and specialist training for members of regional response teams.

(6) Procedures for recovering the costs of a response to a hazardous materials or terrorist incident from persons determined to be responsible for the emergency.

(7) Procedures for bidding and contracting for the provision of a hazmat team for the regional response program.

(8) Criteria for evaluating bids for the provision of a hazmat team for regional response.

(9) Delineation of the roles of the regional response team, local fire department and local public safety personnel, the Division of Emergency Management's area coordinator, and other State agency personnel responding to the scene of a hazardous materials or terrorist incident.

(b) In developing the program and adopting rules, the Secretary shall consult with the Regional Response Team Advisory Committee established pursuant to G.S. 166A-24. (1993 (Reg. Sess., 1994), c. 769, s. 22.4(b); 2002-179, s. 21(c).)

§ 166A-23. Contracts; equipment loans.

(a) The Secretary may contract with any unit or units of local government for the provision of a regional response team to implement the regional response program. Contracts are to be let consistent with the bidding and contract standards and procedures adopted pursuant to G.S. 166A-22(a)(7) and (8). In entering into contracts with units of local government, the Secretary may agree to provide:

(1) A loan of equipment, including a hazmat vehicle, necessary for the provision technician-level entry capability;

(2) Reimbursement of personnel costs when a regional response team is authorized by the Department to respond to a hazmat or terrorist incident, including the cost of call-back personnel;

(3) Reimbursement for use of equipment and vehicles owned by the regional response team;

(4) Replacement of disposable materials and damaged equipment;

(5) Costs of medical surveillance for members of the regional response team, including baseline, maintenance, and exit physicals;

(6) Training expenses; and

(7) Other provisions agreed to by the Secretary and the regional response team.

(b) The Secretary shall not agree to provide reimbursement for:

(1) Costs of clean-up activities, after a spill or leak has been contained;

(2) Local response not requiring technician-level entry capability; or

(3) Standby time.

(c) Any contract entered into between the Secretary and a unit of local government for the provision of a regional response team shall specify that the members of the regional response team, when performing their duties under the contract, shall not be employees of the State and shall not be entitled to benefits under the Teachers' and State Employees' Retirement System or for the payment by the State of federal social security, employment insurance, or workers' compensation.

(d) Regional response teams that have the use of a State hazmat vehicle may use the vehicle for local purposes. Where a State vehicle is used for purposes other than authorized regional response to a hazardous materials or terrorist incident, the regional response team shall be liable for repairs or replacements directly attributable to the nonauthorized response. (1993 (Reg. Sess., 1994), c. 769, s. 22.4(b); 2002-179, s. 21(d).)

§ 166A-24. Immunity of Regional Response Team Personnel.

Members of a regional response team shall be protected from liability under the provisions of G.S. 166A-19.60(a) while responding to a hazardous materials or terrorist incident pursuant to authorization from the Division of Emergency Management. (1993 (Reg. Sess., 1994), c. 769, s. 22.4(b); 2002-179, s. 21(e); 2012-12, s. 2(y).)

§ 166A-25. Right of entry.

A regional response team, when authorized to respond to a release or threatened release of hazardous materials or when authorized to respond to a terrorist or threatened or imminent terrorist incident, may enter onto any private or public property on which the release or terrorist incident has occurred or on which there is an imminent threat of such release or terrorist incident. A regional response team may also enter, under such circumstances, any adjacent or surrounding property in order to respond to the release or threatened release of hazardous material or to monitor, control, and contain the release or perform any other action in mitigation of a hazardous materials or terrorist incident. (1993 (Reg. Sess., 1994), c. 769, s. 22.4(b); 2002-179, s. 21(f).)

§ 166A-26. Regional Response Team Advisory Committee.

(a)   The Regional Response Team Advisory Committee is created. The Secretary shall appoint the members of the Committee and shall designate the chair. In making appointments, the Secretary shall take into consideration the expertise of the appointees in the management of hazardous materials emergencies. The Secretary shall appoint one representative from:

(1)   The Division of Emergency Management;

(2)   The North Carolina Highway Patrol;

(3)   The State Fire and Rescue Commission of the Department of Insurance;

(4)   The Department of Environment and Natural Resources;

(5)   The Department of Transportation;

(6)   The Department of Agriculture and Consumer Services;

(7)   The Chemical Industry Council of North Carolina;

(8)   The N.C. Association of Hazardous Materials Responders;

(9)   Each regional response team;

(10)   The State Bureau of Investigation.

In addition to the persons listed above, the Secretary shall appoint to the Advisory Committee three persons designated jointly by the North Carolina Fire Chiefs Association and the North Carolina State Firemen's Association.

(b) The Advisory Committee shall meet on the call of the chair, or at the request of the Secretary; provided that the Committee shall meet no less than once every three months. The Department of Public Safety shall provide space for the Advisory Committee to meet. The Department also shall provide the Advisory Committee with necessary support staff and supplies to enable the Committee to carry out its duties in an effective manner.

(c) Members of the Advisory Committee shall serve without pay, but shall receive travel allowance, lodging, subsistence, and per diem as provided by G.S. 138-5.

(d) The Regional Response Team Advisory Committee shall advise the Secretary on the establishment of the program for regional response to hazardous materials emergencies in the State. The Committee shall also evaluate and advise the Secretary of the need for additional regional response teams to serve the State. (1993 (Reg. Sess., 1994), c. 769, s. 22.4(b); 1997-261, s. 108; 1997-443, s. 11A.123; 2002-179, s. 21(g); 2011-145, s. 19.1(g).)

§ 166A-27. Action for the recovery of costs of hazardous materials emergency response.

(a) A person who causes the release of a hazardous material requiring the activation of a regional response team shall be liable for all reasonable costs incurred by the regional response team in responding to and mitigating the incident. The Secretary shall invoice the person liable for the hazardous materials release, and, in the event of nonpayment, may institute an action to recover those costs in the superior court of the county in which the release occurred.

(b) A person who causes the release of a hazardous material that results in the activation of one or more State Medical Assistance Teams (SMATs) or the Epidemiology Section of the Division of Public Health of the Department of Health and Human Services shall be liable for all reasonable costs incurred by each team or the Epidemiology Section that responds to or mitigates the incident. The Secretary of Health and Human Services shall invoice the person liable for the hazardous materials release and, in the event of nonpayment, may institute an action to recover those costs in the superior court of the county in which the release occurred. (1993 (Reg. Sess., 1994), c. 769, s. 22.4(b); 2007-107, s. 3.1(a).)

§ 166A-28. Hazardous Materials Emergency Response Fund.

There is established in the Department of Public Safety a fund for those monies collected pursuant to G.S. 166A-27. The Fund is also authorized to accept any gift, grant, or donation of money or property to facilitate the establishment and operation of the regional response system. (1993 (Reg. Sess., 1994), c. 769, s. 22.4(b); 2011-145, s. 19.1(g).)

§ 166A-29. Emergency planning; charge.

(a)   Every person, firm, corporation or municipality who is licensed to construct or who is operating a fixed nuclear facility for the production of electricity shall pay to the Department of Public Safety an annual fee of at least thirty thousand dollars ($30,000) for each fixed nuclear facility which is located within this State or has a Plume Exposure Pathway Emergency Planning Zone of which any part is located within this State. This fee is to be applied to the costs of planning and implementing emergency response activities as are required by the Federal Emergency Management Agency for the operation of nuclear facilities. Said fee is to be paid no later than July 31 of each year. This minimum fee may be increased from time to time as the costs of such planning and implementation increase. Such increases shall be by agreement between the State and the licensees or operators of the fixed nuclear facilities.

(b)   Every person, firm, corporation or municipality who is licensed to construct or who is operating a fixed nuclear facility for the production of electricity shall pay to the Department of Public Safety, for the use of the Radiation Protection Section of the Division of Public Health of the Department of Health and Human Services, an annual fee of thirty-six thousand dollars ($36,000) for each fixed nuclear facility that is located within this State or that has a Plume Exposure Pathway Emergency Planning Zone any part of which is located within this State. This fee shall be applied only to the costs of planning and implementing emergency response activities as required by the Federal Emergency Management Agency for the operation of nuclear facilities. This fee is to be paid no later than July 31 of each year.

(c)   The fees imposed by this section do not revert at the end of a fiscal year. The amount of fees carried forward from one fiscal year to the next shall be taken into consideration in determining the fee to be assessed each fixed nuclear facility under subsection (a) in that fiscal year. (1981, c. 1128, ss. 1, 2; 1983, c. 622, ss. 1-3; 1989, c. 727, s. 219(42); 1989 (Reg. Sess., 1990), c. 964,

s. 1; 1991 (Reg. Sess., 1992), c. 1039, s. 18; 1997-443, s. 11A.123; 2000-109, s. 6; 2002-70, s. 5; 2011-145, ss. 13.3(ooo), 19.1(g); 2012-12, s. 1(a).)

Article 3.

Disaster Service Volunteer Leave Act.

§ 166A-30. Short title.

This act may be cited as the Disaster Service Volunteer Leave Act. (1993, c. 13, s. 1.)

§ 166A-31. Definitions.

As used in this Article:

(1)   "Certified disaster service volunteer" means a person who has completed the necessary training for and been certified as a disaster service specialist by the American National Red Cross.

(2)   "Disaster" means a disaster designated at Level III or higher in the American National Red Cross Regulations and Procedures.

(3)   "State agency" means and includes all departments, institutions, commissions, committees, boards, divisions, bureaus, officers, and officials of the State, including those within the legislative and judicial branches of State government. (1993, c. 13, s. 1.)

§ 166A-32. Disaster service volunteer leave.

An employee of a State agency who is a disaster service volunteer of the American Red Cross may be granted leave from his work with pay for a time not to exceed 15 work days in any 12-month period to participate in specialized disaster relief services for the American Red Cross. To be granted leave, the request for the services of that employee must come from the American Red Cross. The decision to grant the employee leave rests in the sole discretion of the employing State agency based on the work needs of that agency. Employees granted leave pursuant to this Article shall not lose seniority, pay, vacation time, sick time, or earned overtime accumulation. The State agency shall compensate an employee granted leave under this Article at the regular rate of pay for those regular work hours during which the employee is absent from his work. Leave under this Article shall be granted only for services related to a disaster occurring within the United States.

The State of North Carolina shall not be liable for workers compensation claims arising from accident or injury while the State employee is on assignment as a disaster service volunteer for the American Red Cross. Duties performed while on disaster leave shall not be considered to be a work assignment by a state agency. The employee is granted leave based on the need for the employee's area of expertise. Job functions although similar or related are performed on behalf of and for the benefit of the American Red Cross. (1993, c. 13, s. 1; 2001-508, s. 6.)

§ 166A-33: Reserved for future codification purposes.

§ 166A-34: Reserved for future codification purposes.

§ 166A-35: Reserved for future codification purposes.

§ 166A-36: Reserved for future codification purposes.

§ 166A-37: Reserved for future codification purposes.

§ 166A-38: Reserved for future codification purposes.

§ 166A-39: Reserved for future codification purposes.

Article 4.

Emergency Management Assistance Compact.

§ 166A-40. Title of Article; entering into Compact.

(a)   This Article may be cited as the Emergency Management Assistance Compact.

(b) The Emergency Management Assistance Compact, hereinafter "Compact", is hereby enacted into law and entered into by this State with all other states legally joining therein, in the form substantially as set forth in this Article. This Compact is made and entered into by and between the party states which enact this Compact. For the purposes of this Article, the term "states" means the several states, the Commonwealth of Puerto Rico, the District of Columbia, and all United States territorial possessions and the term "party states" means the participating member states which enact and enter into this Compact. (1997-152, s. 1.)

§ 166A-41. Purposes and authorities.

(a) The purpose of this Compact is to provide for mutual assistance between the party states in managing any emergency or disaster that is duly declared by the governor of the affected state or states, whether arising from natural disaster, technological hazard, man-made disaster, civil emergency aspects of resources shortages, community disorders, insurgency, or enemy attack.

(b) This Compact shall also provide for mutual cooperation in emergency-related exercises, testing, or other training activities using equipment and personnel simulating performance of any aspect of the giving and receiving of aid by party states or subdivisions of party states during emergencies, such actions occurring outside actual declared emergency periods. Mutual assistance in this Compact may include the use of the states' National Guard forces, either in accordance with the National Guard Mutual Assistance Compact or by mutual agreement between states. (1997-152, s. 1; 2009-281, s. 1.)

§ 166A-42. General implementation.

(a) Each party state recognizes that many emergencies transcend political jurisdictional boundaries and that intergovernmental coordination is essential in managing these and other emergencies under this Compact. Each party state further recognizes that there will be emergencies that require immediate access and present procedures to apply outside resources to respond to emergencies effectively and promptly. This is because few, if any, individual states have all the resources that they may need in all types of emergencies or the capability of delivering resources to areas where emergencies exist.

(b) The prompt, full, and effective utilization of resources of the participating states, including any resources on hand or available from the federal government or any other source, that are essential to the safety, care, and welfare of the people in the event of any emergency or disaster declared by a party state, shall be the underlying principle on which all articles of this Compact shall be understood.

(c) On behalf of the governor of each party state, the legally designated state official who is assigned responsibility for emergency management shall be responsible for formulation of the appropriate interstate mutual aid plans and procedures necessary to implement this Compact. (1997-152, s. 1.)

§ 166A-43. Party state responsibilities.

(a) It shall be the responsibility of each party state to formulate procedural plans and programs for interstate cooperation in the performance of the responsibilities listed in this Article. In formulating the plans, and in carrying them out, the party states, insofar as practicable, shall:

(1) Review individual state hazards analyses and, to the extent reasonably possible, determine all those potential emergencies the party state might jointly suffer, whether due to natural disaster, technological hazard, man-made disaster, emergency aspects of resource shortages, civil disorders, insurgency, or enemy attack.

(2) Review the party states' individual emergency plans and develop a plan that will determine the mechanism for the interstate management and provision of assistance concerning any potential emergency.

(3) Develop interstate procedures to fill any identified gaps and to resolve any identified inconsistencies or overlaps in existing or developed plans.

(4) Assist in warning communities adjacent to or crossing the state boundaries.

(5) Protect and assure uninterrupted delivery of services, medicines, water, food, energy and fuel, search and rescue, and critical lifeline equipment services, and resources, both human and material.

(6)   Inventory and set procedures for the interstate loan and delivery of human and material resources, together with procedures for reimbursement or forgiveness.

(7)   Provide, to the extent authorized by law, for temporary suspension of any statutes or ordinances that restrict the implementation of the above responsibilities.

(b)   The authorized representative of a party state may request assistance of another party state by contacting the authorized representative of that state. The provisions of this Compact shall only apply to requests for assistance made by and to authorized representatives. Requests may be verbal or in writing. If verbal, the request shall be confirmed in writing within 30 days of the verbal request. Requests shall provide the following information:

(1)   A description of the emergency service function for which assistance is needed, including fire services, law enforcement, emergency medical, transportation, communications, public works and engineering, building inspection, planning and information assistance, mass care, resource support, health and medical services, and search and rescue.

(2)   The amount and type of personnel, equipment, materials and supplies needed, and a reasonable estimate of the length of time they will be needed.

(3)   The specific place and time for staging of the assisting party's response and a point of contact at that location.

(c)   There shall be frequent consultation between state officials who have assigned emergency management responsibilities and other appropriate representatives of the party states with affected jurisdictions and the federal government, with free exchange of information, plans, and resource records relating to emergency capabilities. (1997-152, s. 1.)

§ 166A-44. Limitations.

(a)   Any party state requested to render mutual aid or conduct exercises and training for mutual aid shall take such action as is necessary to provide and make available the resources covered by this Compact in accordance with the terms hereof; provided that the state rendering aid may withhold resources to the extent necessary to provide reasonable protection for such state.

(b) Each party state shall afford to the emergency forces of any party state while operating within its state limits under the terms and conditions of this Compact, the same powers (except that of arrest unless specifically authorized by the receiving state), duties, rights, and privileges as are afforded forces of the state in which they are performing emergency services. Emergency forces will continue under the command and control of their regular leaders, but the organizational units will come under the operational control of the emergency services authorities of the state receiving assistance. These conditions may be activated, as needed, only subsequent to a declaration of a state of emergency or disaster by the governor of the party state that is to receive assistance or commencement of exercises or training for mutual aid and shall continue so long as the exercises or training for mutual aid are in progress, the state of emergency or disaster remains in effect, or loaned resources remain in the receiving state or states, whichever is longer. (1997-152, s. 1.)

§ 166A-45. Licenses and permits.

Whenever any person holds a license, certificate, or other permit issued by any party state evidencing the meeting of qualifications for professional, mechanical, or other skills, and when assistance is requested by the receiving party state, the person shall be deemed licensed, certified, or permitted by the state requesting assistance to render aid involving skill to meet a declared emergency or disaster, subject to any limitations and conditions the governor of the requesting state may prescribe by executive order or otherwise. (1997-152, s. 1.)

§ 166A-46. Liability.

Officers or employees of a party state rendering aid in another state pursuant to this Compact shall be considered agents of the requesting state for tort liability and immunity purposes; and no party state or its officers or employees rendering aid in another state pursuant to this Compact shall be liable for any act or omission occurring as a result of a good faith attempt to render aid or as a result of the use of any equipment or supplies used in connection with an attempt to render aid. For the purposes of this Article, "good faith" does not include willful misconduct, gross negligence, or recklessness. (1997-152, s. 1; 2007-484, s. 24.)

§ 166A-47. Supplementary agreements.

Inasmuch as it is probable that the pattern and detail of the machinery for mutual aid among two or more states may differ from that among the states that are party hereto, this instrument contains elements of a broad base common to all states, and nothing herein contained shall preclude any state from entering into supplementary agreements with another state or affect any other agreements already in force between states. Supplementary agreements may comprehend, but shall not be limited to, provisions for evacuation and reception of injured and other persons and the exchange of medical, fire, police, public utility, reconnaissance, welfare, transportation and communications personnel, and equipment and supplies. (1997-152, s. 1.)

§ 166A-48. Compensation.

Each party state shall provide for the payment of compensation and death benefits to injured members of the emergency forces of that state and representatives of deceased members of the forces in case the members sustain injuries or are killed while rendering aid pursuant to this Compact, in the same manner and on the same terms as if the injury or death were sustained within their own state. (1997-152, s. 1.)

§ 166A-49. Reimbursement.

Any party state rendering aid in another state pursuant to this Compact shall be reimbursed by the party state receiving the aid for any loss or damage to or expense incurred in the operation of any equipment and the provision of any service in answering a request for aid and for the costs incurred in connection with the requests; provided, that any aiding party state may assume in whole or in part the loss, damage, expense, or other cost, or may loan the equipment or donate the services to the receiving party state without charge or cost; and provided further, that any two or more party states may enter into supplementary agreements establishing a different allocation of costs among those states. (1997-152, s. 1.)

§ 166A-50. Evacuation.

Plans for the orderly evacuation and interstate reception of portions of the civilian population as the result of any emergency or disaster of sufficient proportions to so warrant shall be worked out and maintained between the party states and the emergency management or services directors of the various jurisdictions where any type of incident requiring evacuations might occur. Plans shall be put into effect by request of the state from which evacuees come and shall include the manner of transporting the evacuees, the number of evacuees to be received in different areas, the manner in which food, clothing, housing, and medical care will be provided, the registration of the evacuees, the providing of facilities for the notification of relatives or friends, and the forwarding of the evacuees to other areas or the bringing in of additional materials, supplies, and all other relevant factors. The plans shall provide that the party state receiving evacuees and the party state from which the evacuees come shall mutually agree as to reimbursement of out-of-pocket expenses incurred in receiving and caring for evacuees, for expenditures for transportation, food, clothing, medicines and medical care, and like items. The expenditures shall be reimbursed as agreed by the party state from which the evacuees come and that party state shall assume the responsibility for the ultimate support of repatriation of the evacuees. (1997-152, s. 1.)

§ 166A-51. Effective date.

(a) This Compact shall become operative immediately upon its enactment into law by any two states; thereafter, this Compact shall become effective as to any other state upon its enactment by the state.

(b) Any party state may withdraw from this Compact by enacting a statute repealing the same, but no withdrawal shall take effect until 30 days after the governor of the withdrawing state has given notice in writing of the withdrawal to the governors of all other party states. The action shall not relieve the withdrawing state from obligations assumed hereunder prior to the effective date of withdrawal.

(c) Duly authenticated copies of this Compact and of any supplementary agreements as may be entered into shall, at the time of their approval, be deposited with each of the party states and with the Federal Emergency Management Agency and other appropriate agencies of the federal government. (1997-152, s. 1.)
§ 166A-52. Validity.

If any provision of this Compact is declared unconstitutional, or the applicability thereof to any person or circumstances is held invalid, the constitutionality of the remainder of this act and the applicability thereof to other persons and circumstances shall not be affected thereby. (1997-152, s. 1.)

§ 166A-53. Additional provisions.

Nothing in this Compact shall authorize or permit the use of military force by the National Guard of a state at any place outside that state in any emergency for which the President is authorized by law to call into federal service the militia, or for any purpose for which the use of the Army or the Air Force would in the absence of express statutory authorization be prohibited under section 1385 of Title 18, United States Code. (1997-152, s. 1; 2009-281, s. 1.)

§ 166A-54. Reserved for future codification purposes.

§ 166A-55. Reserved for future codification purposes.

§ 166A-56. Reserved for future codification purposes.

§ 166A-57. Reserved for future codification purposes.

§ 166A-58. Reserved for future codification purposes.

§ 166A-59. Reserved for future codification purposes.

Article 5.

Emergency Management Certification Program.

§ 166A-60. Emergency Management Certification Program authority; purpose.

The Division of Emergency Management in the Department of Public Safety shall establish, as a voluntary program, an Emergency Management Certification Program as provided for in this Article. The purpose of the Program is to strengthen and enhance the professional competencies of emergency management personnel in State and local emergency management agencies. (2009-192, s. 2; 2011-145, s. 19.1(g).)

§ 166A-61. Program standards and guidelines.

(a) The Division shall establish standards and guidelines for administration of the Program, including:

(1) Minimum educational and training standards that must be met in order to qualify for Type IV (entry), Type III (basic), Type II (intermediate), and Type I (advanced) emergency management certification.

(2) Levels of education or equivalent experience that may be met in order to qualify for the certifications provided for in subdivision (1) of this subsection.

(3) Levels of education or equivalent experience for instructors who participate in programs or courses of instruction.

(4) Curricula, syllabi, and other educational materials.

(5) Mode(s) of delivery of educational and training programs.

(b) In developing the Program, the Division may consult and cooperate with political subdivisions, agencies of the State, other governmental agencies, universities, colleges, community colleges, and other institutions, public or private, concerning the development of the Program and a systematic career development plan, including conducting and stimulating research by public and private agencies designed to improve education and training in the administration of emergency management.

(c) The Division shall study and make reports and recommendations to the Secretary of Public Safety and other appropriate agencies and officials concerning compliance with federal guidance, training, educational, technical assistance needs, and equipment needs of State and local emergency management agencies. (2009-192, s. 2; 2011-145, s. 19.1(g).)

§ 166A-62. Emergency Management Training and Standards Advisory Board.

(a) The Secretary of Public Safety shall establish and appoint the Emergency Management Training and Standards Advisory Board to provide oversight of training and certification programs established pursuant to this Article.

(b) The composition of the Board shall include emergency management subject matter experts representative of the State, its political subdivisions, and private industry.

(c) The duties of the Board shall include:

(1) Oversight of the Emergency Management Certification Program.

(2) Review of applications for certification.

(3) Issuance of certifications at least semiannually.

(d) The Board shall meet at least semiannually and at other times at the discretion of the Secretary. (2009-192, s. 2; 2011-145, s. 19.1(g).)

§ 166A-63. Issuance of certification; reciprocity; renewal.

(a) The Emergency Management Training and Standards Advisory Board shall issue documentation of certification, in a form and manner prescribed by the Division, to each applicant within North Carolina demonstrating successful completion of the requirements for the level of certification sought by the applicant.

(b) The Board may issue documentation of certification to any person in another state or territory if the person's qualifications were, at the date of registration or certification, substantially equivalent to the requirements established pursuant to this Article.

(c) Every person certified pursuant to this Article who desires to maintain certification shall apply for renewal of certification within five years of the date of original certification or certification renewal.

(d) Renewal of Type I (advanced) certification is subject to completion of at least 24 hours of continuing education requirements as established by the Board.

(e) A certification that is not renewed in accordance with this section automatically expires. The Board may approve reinstatement of an expired certification upon good cause shown by the applicant.

(f) Certifications that have been expired for more than five years shall not be reinstated. (2009-192, s. 2.)

Chapter 167

State Civil Air Patrol.

§§ 167-1 through 167-3: Repealed by Session Laws 1973, c. 620, s. 9.

Chapter 168

Persons with Disabilities.

Article 1.

Rights.

§ 168-1. Purpose and definition.

The State shall encourage and enable persons with disabilities to participate fully in the social and economic life of the State and to engage in remunerative employment. For purposes of this Article, the term "person with a disability" shall have the same meaning as set forth in G.S. 168A-3(7a). (1973, c. 493, s. 1; 2000-121, s. 33; 2005-450, s. 1.)

§ 168-2. Right of access to and use of public places.

Persons with disabilities have the same right as persons without disabilities to the full and free use of the streets, highways, sidewalks, walkways, public buildings, public facilities, and all other buildings and facilities, both publicly and privately owned, which serve the public. The Department of Health and Human Services shall develop, print, and promote the publication ACCESS NORTH CAROLINA. It shall make copies of the publication available to the Department of Commerce for its use in Welcome Centers and other appropriate Department of Commerce offices. The Department of Commerce shall promote ACCESS NORTH CAROLINA in its publications (including providing a toll-free telephone line and an address for requesting copies of the publication) and provide technical assistance to the Department of Health and Human Services on travel attractions to be included in ACCESS NORTH CAROLINA. The Department of Commerce shall forward all requests for mailing ACCESS NORTH CAROLINA to the Department of Health and Human Services. (1973, c. 493, s. 1; 1991, c. 672, s. 4; c. 726, s. 23; 1991 (Reg. Sess., 1992), c. 959, s. 84; 1997-443, s. 11A.118(a); 2004-203, s. 61; 2005-450, s. 1.)

§ 168-3. Right to use of public conveyances, accommodations, etc.

Persons with disabilities are entitled to accommodations, advantages, facilities, and privileges of all common carriers, airplanes, motor vehicles, railroad trains, motor buses, streetcars, boats, or any other public conveyances or modes of transportation; hotels, lodging places, places of public accommodation, amusement or resort to which the general public is invited, subject only to the conditions and limitations established by law and applicable alike to all persons. (1973, c. 493, s. 1; 2005-450, s. 1.)

§§ 168-4 through 168-4.1: Repealed by Session Laws 1985, c. 514, s. 1.

§ 168-4.2. May be accompanied by service animal.

(a) Every person with a disability has the right to be accompanied by a service animal trained to assist the person with his or her specific disability in any of the places listed in G.S. 168-3, and has the right to keep the service animal on any premises the person leases, rents, or uses. The person qualifies for these rights upon the showing of a tag, issued by the Department of Health and Human Services, under G.S. 168-4.3, stamped "NORTH CAROLINA SERVICE ANIMAL PERMANENT REGISTRATION" and stamped with a registration number, or upon a showing that the animal is being trained or has been trained as a service animal. The service animal may accompany a person in any of the places listed in G.S. 168-3.

(b) An animal in training to become a service animal may be taken into any of the places listed in G.S. 168-3 for the purpose of training when the animal is accompanied by a person who is training the service animal and the animal wears a collar and leash, harness, or cape that identifies the animal as a service animal in training. The trainer shall be liable for any damage caused by the animal while using a public conveyance or on the premises of a public facility or other place listed in G.S. 168-3. (1985, c. 514, s. 1; 1987, c. 401, s. 1; 1995, c. 276, s. 1; 1997-443, s. 11A.118(a); 2004-203, s. 62(a); 2005-450, s. 1.)

§ 168-4.3. Training and registration of service animal.

The Department of Health and Human Services, shall adopt rules for the registration of service animals and shall issue registrations to a person with a disability who makes application for registration of an animal that serves as a service animal or to a person who is training an animal as a service animal.

The rules adopted regarding registration shall require that the animal be trained or be in training as a service animal. The rules shall provide that the certification and registration need not be renewed while the animal is serving or training with the person applying for the registration. No fee may be charged the person for the application, registration, tag, or replacement in the event the original is lost. The Department of Health and Human Services may, by rule, issue a certification or accept the certification issued by the appropriate training facilities. (1985, c. 514, s. 1; 1987, c. 401, s. 2; 1997-443, s. 11A.118(a); 2004-203, s. 62(b); 2005-450, s. 1.)

§ 168-4.4. Responsibility for service animal.

Neither a person with a disability who is accompanied by a service animal, nor a person who is training a service animal, may be required to pay any extra compensation for the animal. The person has all the responsibilities and liabilities placed on any person by any applicable law when that person owns or uses any animal, including liability for any damage done by the animal. (1985, c. 514, s. 1; 2004-203, s. 62(c); 2005-450, s. 1.)

§ 168-4.5. Penalty.

It is unlawful to disguise an animal as a service animal or service animal in training. It is unlawful to deprive a person with a disability or a person training a service animal of any rights granted the person pursuant to G.S. 168-4.2 through G.S. 168-4.4, or of any rights or privileges granted the general public with respect to being accompanied by animals or to charge any fee for the use of the service animal. Violation of this section shall be a Class 3 misdemeanor.

(1985, c. 514, s. 1; 1987, ch. 401, s. 3; 1993, c. 539, s. 1120; 1994, Ex. Sess., c. 24, s. 14(c); 2005-450, s. 1.)

§ 168-4.6. Donation of dogs for training.

Dogs impounded by a local dog warden that are not redeemed shall be donated to a nonprofit agency engaged in the training of service dogs, upon the agency's request. (1985, c. 514, s. 1; 2005-450, s. 1.)

§ 168-5: Repealed by Session Laws 2005-450, s. 1, effective September 1, 2005.

§ 168-6. Repealed by Session Laws 1985, c. 571, s. 3.

§§ 168-7 through 168-7.1: Repealed by Session Laws 1985, c. 514, s. 1.

§ 168-8. Right to habilitation and rehabilitation services.

A person with a disability shall be entitled to such habilitation and rehabilitation services as available and needed for the development or restoration of their capabilities to the fullest extent possible. Such services shall include, but not be limited to, education, training, treatment and other services to provide for adequate food, clothing, housing and transportation during the course of education, training and treatment. A person with a disability shall be entitled to these rights subject only to the conditions and limitations established by law and applicable alike to all persons. (1973, c. 493, s. 1; 2005-450, s. 1.)

§ 168-9. Right to housing.

Each person with a disability who is a citizen shall have the same right as any other citizen to live and reside in residential communities, homes, and group homes, and no person or group of persons, including governmental bodies or political subdivisions of the State, shall be permitted, or have the authority, to prevent any person with a disability who is a citizen from living and residing in residential communities, homes, and group homes on the same basis and conditions as any other citizen. Nothing herein shall be construed to conflict with provisions of Chapter 122C of the General Statutes. (1975, c. 635; 1985, c. 589, s. 61; 2005-450, s. 1.)

§ 168-10. Eliminate discrimination in treatment of persons with disabilities.

Each person with a disability shall have the same consideration as any other person for individual accident and health insurance coverage, and no insurer, service corporation, multiple employer welfare arrangement, or health maintenance organization subject to Chapter 58 of the General Statutes solely on the basis of the person's disability, shall deny such coverage or benefits. The availability of coverage or benefits shall not be denied solely because of the disability; however, any such insurer may charge the appropriate premiums or fees for the risk insured on the same basis and conditions as insurance issued to other persons, in accordance with actuarial and underwriting principles and other coverage provisions prescribed in Chapter 58 of the General Statutes. No insurer, service corporation, multiple employer welfare arrangement, or health maintenance organization subject to Chapter 58 of the General Statutes shall be prohibited from excluding by waiver or otherwise, any preexisting conditions from coverage as prescribed in G.S. 58-51-15(a)(2)b. (1977, c. 894, ss. 1, 2; 1991, c. 720, s. 80; 1999-219, s. 3.1; 2005-450, s. 1.)

§ 168-11: Reserved for future codification purposes.

§ 168-12: Reserved for future codification purposes.

§ 168-13: Reserved for future codification purposes.

Article 2.

Vocational Rehabilitation.

§ 168-14. Vocational rehabilitation services for deaf persons.

The Department of Health and Human Services shall promote the employment of deaf persons in this State. The Department shall assist deaf persons whose disability limits employment opportunities in obtaining gainful employment commensurate with their abilities and in maintaining such employment.

The Department, in furtherance of these objectives, shall maintain statistics regarding trades and occupations in which deaf persons are employed.

The Department shall attempt to employ deaf persons in its vocational rehabilitation services for deaf persons and shall have at least one deaf person so employed. (1975, c. 412, s. 2; 1997-443, s. 11A.118(a).)

Article 3.

Family Care Homes.

§ 168-20. Public policy.

The General Assembly has declared in Article 1 of this Chapter that it is the public policy of this State to provide persons with disabilities with the opportunity to live in a normal residential environment. (1981, c. 565, s. 1; 2005-450, s. 1.)

§ 168-21. Definitions.

As used in this Article:

(1) "Family care home" means a home with support and supervisory personnel that provides room and board, personal care and habilitation services in a family environment for not more than six resident persons with disabilities.

(2) "Person with disabilities" means a person with a temporary or permanent physical, emotional, or mental disability including but not limited to mental retardation, cerebral palsy, epilepsy, autism, hearing and sight impairments, emotional disturbances and orthopedic impairments but not including mentally ill persons who are dangerous to others as defined in G.S. 122C-3(11)b. (1981, c. 565, s. 1; 1985, c. 589, s. 62; 1995, c. 535, s. 36; 2002-159, s. 24; 2005-450, s. 1.)

§ 168-22. Family care home; zoning and other purposes.

(a) A family care home shall be deemed a residential use of property for zoning purposes and shall be a permissible use in all residential districts of all political subdivisions. No political subdivision may require that a family care home, its owner, or operator obtain, because of the use, a conditional use permit, special use permit, special exception or variance from any such zoning ordinance or plan; provided, however, that a political subdivision may prohibit a family care home from being located within a one-half mile radius of an existing family care home.

(b)   A family care home shall be deemed a residential use of property for the purposes of determining charges or assessments imposed by political subdivisions or businesses for water, sewer, power, telephone service, cable television, garbage and trash collection, repairs or improvements to roads, streets, and sidewalks, and other services, utilities, and improvements. (1981, c. 565, s. 1; 1993 (Reg. Sess., 1994), c. 619, s. 1; 1999-219, s. 3.2.)

§ 168-23. Certain private agreements void.

Any restriction, reservation, condition, exception, or covenant in any subdivision plan, deed, or other instrument of or pertaining to the transfer, sale, lease, or use of property which would permit residential use of property but prohibit the use of such property as a family care home shall, to the extent of such prohibition, be void as against public policy and shall be given no legal or equitable force or effect. (1981, c. 565, s. 1.)

Chapter 168A

Persons With Disabilities Protection Act.

§ 168A-1. Title.

This Chapter may be cited as the North Carolina Persons With Disabilities Protection Act. (1985, c. 571, s. 1; 1999-160, s. 1.)

§ 168A-2. Statement of purpose.

(a)   The purpose of this Chapter is to ensure equality of opportunity, to promote independent living, self-determination, and economic self-sufficiency, and to encourage and enable all persons with disabilities to participate fully to the maximum extent of their abilities in the social and economic life of the State, to engage in remunerative employment, to use available public accommodations and public services, and to otherwise pursue their rights and privileges as inhabitants of this State.

(b) The General Assembly finds that: the practice of discrimination based upon a disabling condition is contrary to the public interest and to the principles of freedom and equality of opportunity; the practice of discrimination on the basis of a disabling condition threatens the rights and proper privileges of the inhabitants of this State; and such discrimination results in a failure to realize the productive capacity of individuals to their fullest extent. (1985, c. 571, s. 1; 1999-160, s. 1; 2002-163, s. 1.)

§ 168A-3. Definitions.

As used in this Chapter, unless the context otherwise requires:

(1) "Covered governmental entity" means any State department, institution, agency, or any political subdivision of the State or any person that contracts with a State department, institution, agency, or political subdivision of the State for the delivery of public services, including, but not limited to, education, health, social services, recreation, and rehabilitation.

(1a) "Disabling condition" means any condition or characteristic that renders a person a person with a disability.

(1b) "Discriminatory practice" means any practice prohibited by this Chapter.

(2) "Employer" means any person employing 15 or more full-time employees within the State, but excluding a person whose only employees are hired to work as domestic or farm workers at that person's home or farm.

(3) "Employment agency" means a person regularly undertaking with or without compensation to procure for employees opportunities to work for an employer and includes an agent of such a person.

(4) Recodified as G.S. 168A-3(7a).

(4a) "Information technology" has the same meaning as in G.S. 147-33.81. The term also specifically includes information transaction machines.

(5) Recodified as G.S. 168A-3(1).

(6) "Labor organization" means an organization of any kind, an agency or employee representation committee, a group association, or a plan, in which employees participate and which exists for the purpose, in whole or in part, of dealing with employers concerning grievances, labor disputes, wages, rates of pay, hours, or other terms or conditions of employment.

(7) "Person" includes any individual, partnership, association, corporation, labor organization, legal representative, trustee, receiver, and the State and its departments, agencies, and political subdivisions.

(7a) "Person with a disability" means any person who (i) has a physical or mental impairment which substantially limits one or more major life activities; (ii) has a record of such an impairment; or (iii) is regarded as having such an impairment. As used in this subdivision, the term:

a. "Physical or mental impairment" means (i) any physiological disorder or abnormal condition, cosmetic disfigurement, or anatomical loss, caused by bodily injury, birth defect or illness, affecting a body system, including, but not limited to, neurological; musculoskeletal; special sense organs; respiratory, including speech organs; cardiovascular; reproductive; digestive; genitourinary; hemic and lymphatic; skin; and endocrine; or (ii) any mental disorder, such as mental retardation, organic brain syndrome, mental illness, specific learning disabilities, and other developmental disabilities, but (iii) excludes (A) sexual preferences; (B) active alcoholism or drug addiction or abuse; and (C) any disorder, condition or disfigurement which is temporary in nature, lasting six months or fewer, and leaving no residual impairment. A disorder, condition, or disfigurement that is episodic or in remission is a physical or mental impairment if it would substantially limit a major life activity when active.

b. "Major life activities" means functions, including, but not limited to, caring for one's self, performing manual tasks, walking, seeing, hearing, speaking, eating, sleeping, lifting, bending, standing, breathing, learning, reading, concentrating, thinking, communicating, and working. A major life activity also includes the operation of a major bodily function, including, but not limited to, functions of the immune system, normal cell growth, and digestive, bowel, bladder, neurological, brain, respiratory, circulatory, endocrine, and reproductive functions.

c. "Has a record of such an impairment" means has a history of, or has been misclassified as having, a mental or physical impairment that substantially limits major life activities.

d. "Is regarded as having an impairment" means (i) has a physical or mental impairment that does not substantially limit major life activities but that is treated as constituting such a limitation; (ii) has a physical or mental impairment that substantially limits major life activities because of the attitudes of others; or (iii) has none of the impairments defined in paragraph a. of this subdivision but is treated as having such an impairment.

The determination of whether an impairment substantially limits a major life activity shall be made without regard to the ameliorative effects of mitigating measures, such as (i) medication, medical supplies, equipment, or appliances, low-vision devices, which do not include ordinary eyeglasses or contact lenses, prosthetics, including limbs and devices, hearing aids and cochlear implants or other implantable hearing devices, mobility devices, or oxygen therapy equipment and supplies; (ii) use of assistive technology; (iii) reasonable accommodations or auxiliary aids or services; or (iv) learned behavioral or adaptive neurological modifications.

(8) "Place of public accommodations" includes, but is not limited to, any place, facility, store, other establishment, hotel, or motel, which supplies goods or services on the premises to the public or which solicits or accepts the patronage or trade of any person.

(9) "Qualified person with a disability" means:

a. With regard to employment, a person with a disability who can satisfactorily perform the duties of the job in question, with or without reasonable accommodation, (i) provided that the person with a disability shall not be held to standards of performance different from other employees similarly employed, and (ii) further provided that the disabling condition does not create an unreasonable risk to the safety or health of the person with a disability, other employees, the employer's customers, or the public;

b. With regard to places of public accommodation a person with a disability who can benefit from the goods or services provided by the place of public accommodation; and

c. With regard to public services and public transportation a person with a disability who meets prerequisites for participation that are uniformly applied to all participants, such as income or residence, and that do not have the effect of discriminating against persons with a disability.

(10) "Reasonable accommodations" means:

a. With regard to employment, making reasonable physical changes in the workplace, including, but not limited to, making facilities accessible, modifying equipment and providing mechanical aids to assist in operating equipment, or making reasonable changes in the duties of the job in question that would accommodate the known disabling conditions of the person with a disability seeking the job in question by enabling him or her to satisfactorily perform the duties of that job; provided that "reasonable accommodation" does not require that an employer:

1. Hire one or more employees, other than the person with a disability, for the purpose, in whole or in part, of enabling the person with a disability to be employed; or

2. Reassign duties of the job in question to other employees without assigning to the employee with a disability duties that would compensate for those reassigned; or

3. Reassign duties of the job in question to one or more other employees where such reassignment would increase the skill, effort or responsibility required of such other employee or employees from that required prior to the change in duties; or

4. Alter, modify, change or deviate from bona fide seniority policies or practices; or

5. Provide accommodations of a personal nature, including, but not limited to, eyeglasses, hearing aids, or prostheses, except under the same terms and conditions as such items are provided to the employer's employees generally; or

6. Repealed by Session Laws 2002-163, s. 2, effective January 1, 2003.

7. Make any changes that would impose on the employer an undue hardship.

b. With regard to a place of public accommodations and a covered governmental entity, making reasonable efforts to accommodate the disabling conditions of a person with a disability, including, but not limited to, making facilities accessible to and usable by persons with a disability, redesigning equipment, providing auxiliary aids and services needed to make aurally and visually delivered materials available, as needed, to individuals with hearing or sight impairments, providing mechanical aids or other assistance, or using alternative accessible locations, provided that reasonable accommodations does not require efforts which would impose an undue hardship on the entity involved.

(11) "Undue hardship" means a significant difficulty or expense. The following factors shall be considered in determining whether an accommodation would impose an undue hardship:

a. The nature and cost of the accommodations needed under this Chapter.

b. The overall financial resources of the particular facility or facilities involved in the provision of the accommodation, the number of persons employed at the facility, the effect on expenses and resources at the facility, and any other impact on the operation of the facility.

c. The overall effect on the financial resources of the covered entity, the number of persons employed by the covered entity, and the number, type, and location of the covered entity's facilities.

d. The type of operations of the covered entity, including the composition, structure, and functions of the workforce of the entity, the geographic separateness of the particular facility to the covered entity, and the administrative or fiscal relationship of the particular facility to the covered entity. (1985, c. 571, s. 1; 1999-160, s. 1; 1999-456, s. 44; 2002-163, s. 2; 2011-94, s. 1.)

§ 168A-4. Reasonable accommodation duties.

(a) A qualified person with a disability requesting a reasonable accommodation must apprise the employer, employment agency, labor organization, place of public accommodation, or covered governmental entity of his or her disabling condition, submit any necessary medical documentation, make suggestions for such possible accommodations as are known to such person with a disability, and cooperate in any ensuing discussion and evaluation aimed at determining possible or feasible accommodations.

(b)   Once a qualified person with a disability has requested an accommodation, or if a potential accommodation is obvious in the circumstances, an employer, employment agency, labor organization, place of public accommodation, or covered governmental entity shall investigate whether there are reasonable accommodations that can be made and make reasonable accommodations as defined in G.S. 168A-3(10). (1985, c. 571, s. 1; 1999-160, s. 1; 2011-94, s. 2.)

§ 168A-5. Discrimination in employment; exemptions.

(a)   Discriminatory practices. - It is a discriminatory practice for:

(1)   An employer to fail to hire or consider for employment or promotion, to discharge, or otherwise to discriminate against a qualified person with a disability on the basis of a disabling condition with respect to compensation or the terms, conditions, or privileges of employment;

(2)   An employment agency to fail or refuse to refer for employment, or otherwise to discriminate against a qualified person with a disability on the basis of a disabling condition;

(3)   A person controlling an apprenticeship, on-the-job, or other training or retraining program, to discriminate against a qualified person with a disability on the basis of a disabling condition in admission to, or employment in, a program established to provide apprenticeship or other training;

(4)   An employer or employment agency to require an applicant to identify himself as a person with a disability prior to a conditional offer of employment; however, any employer may invite an applicant to identify himself as a person with a disability in order to act affirmatively on his behalf; or

(5)   An employer, labor organization, or employment agency to fail to meet the duties imposed on them by G.S. 168A-4(b).

(b)   Exemptions. - It is not a discriminatory action for an employer, employment agency, or labor organization:

(1) To make an employment decision on the basis of State and federal laws or regulations imposing physical, health, mental or psychological job requirements;

(2) To fail to hire, transfer or promote, or to discharge a person with a disability who has a history of drug abuse or who is unlawfully using drugs where the job in question is in an establishment that manufactures, distributes, dispenses, conducts research, stores, sells or otherwise handles controlled substances regulated by the North Carolina Controlled Substances Act, G.S. 90-86 et seq.;

(3) To fail to hire, transfer, or promote, or to discharge a person with a disability because the person has a communicable disease which would disqualify a person without a disability from similar employment;

(4) To fail to make reasonable accommodations where the person with a disability has not fulfilled the duties imposed by G.S. 168A-4;

(5) To inquire whether a person has the ability to perform the duties of the job in question;

(6) To require or request a person to undergo a medical examination, which may include a medical history, for the purpose of determining the person's ability or capacity to safely and satisfactorily perform the duties of available jobs for which the person is otherwise qualified, or to aid in determining possible accommodations for a disabling condition, provided (i) that an offer of employment has been made on the condition that the person meets the physical and mental requirements of the job with or without reasonable accommodation; and (ii) that the examination, unless limited to determining the extent to which a person's disabling condition would interfere with his or her ability or capacity to safely and satisfactorily perform the duties of the job in question or the possible accommodations for a disabling condition, is required of all persons conditionally offered employment for the same position regardless of disabling condition;

(7) To obtain medical information or to require or request a medical examination where such information or examination is for the purpose of establishing an employee health record;

(8) To administer pre-employment tests, provided that the tests (i) measure only job-related abilities, (ii) are required of all applicants for the same position

unless such tests are limited to determining the extent to which the person's disabling condition would interfere with his or her ability to safely and satisfactorily perform the duties of the job in question or the possible accommodations for the job in question, and (iii) accurately measure the applicant's aptitude, achievement level, or whatever factors they purport to measure rather than reflecting the impaired sensory, manual or speaking skills of a person with a disability except when those skills are requirements of the job in question, provided that an employer shall not be liable for improper testing which was administered by a State agency acting as an employment agency. (1985, c. 571, s. 1; 1999-160, s. 1.)

§ 168A-6. Discrimination in public accommodations.

It is a discriminatory practice for a person to deny a qualified person with a disability the full and equal enjoyment of the goods, services, facilities, privileges, advantages, and accommodations of a place of public accommodation on the basis of a disabling condition. In the area of structural modifications, this section may be satisfied by compliance with the North Carolina Building Code. (1985, c. 571, s. 1; 1999-160, s. 1.)

§ 168A-7. Discrimination in public service.

(a)   It is a discriminatory practice for a covered governmental entity to exclude a qualified person with a disability from participation in or deny the benefits of services, programs, or activities because of a disability or to refuse to provide reasonable accommodations, including auxiliary aids and services necessary for a known qualified person with a disability to use or benefit from existing public services operated by such entity; provided that the accommodations do not impose an undue hardship on the entity involved. This subsection includes equivalent services provided via information technology.

(b)   A covered governmental entity shall administer its services, programs, and activities in the most integrated setting appropriate to the needs of persons with disabilities. (1985, c. 571, s. 1; 1999-160, s. 1; 2002-163, s. 3; 2011-94, s. 3.)

§ 168A-8. Discrimination in public transportation.

It is a discriminatory practice for any transportation system providing transportation to the general public to fail to ensure access to and the benefits of public transportation to a qualified person with a disability; however, public transportation systems may use alternative methods to provide transportation for persons with a disability, as long as persons with a disability are offered transportation that, in relation to the transportation offered to other persons, is:

(1) In a similar geographic area of operation;

(2) For fares not greater in price;

(3) With similar or no restrictions as to trip purpose;

(4) With reasonable response time; and

(5) With similar hours of operations.

Nothing in this section shall apply to privately owned, local transit or transportation systems existing on October 1, 1985, or to interstate air carriers complying with federal regulations promulgated by the Civil Aeronautics Board and administered by the United States Department of Transportation. (1985, c. 571, s. 1; 1999-160, s. 1.)

§ 168A-9. Affirmative defenses.

Any employer may assert affirmative defenses in any action brought under this Chapter. This section shall not create any inference that an employment action which is not listed as an affirmative defense is therefore, by implication, a discriminatory practice, so long as the employment action is not otherwise prohibited by this Chapter. The following is a non-exclusive list of affirmative defenses:

(1) The failure of the qualified person with a disability to comply with or meet the employer's work rules and policies or performance standards, absent a reasonable accommodation excusing noncompliance, provided that the person is not held to rules or standards different from other employees without a disability similarly employed;

(2) The excessive, willful or habitual tardiness or absence of a qualified person with a disability, absent a reasonable accommodation that allows for

flexible working hours, provided that the standard used by the employer in determining whether such tardiness or absence is excessive is the same as that applied by the employer to employees without a disability similarly employed; or

(3)   A bona fide seniority or merit system, or a system which measures earnings by quantity or quality of work or production, or differences in location of employment. (1985, c. 571, s. 1; 1999-160, s. 1; 2011-94, s. 4.)

§ 168A-10. Retaliation prohibited.

(a)   No employer shall discharge, expel, refuse to hire, or otherwise discriminate against any person or applicant for employment, nor shall any employment agency discriminate against any person, nor shall a labor organization discriminate against any member or applicant for membership because the person has opposed any practice made a discriminatory practice by this Chapter or because the person has testified, assisted or participated in any manner in proceedings under this Chapter.

(b)   No entity or person covered under this Chapter shall retaliate against or coerce, intimidate, threaten, or interfere with a person who exercises rights under this Chapter or assists a person in exercising the person's rights under this Chapter. (1985, c. 571, s. 1; 2011-94, s. 5.)

§ 168A-10.1. Dispute resolution in public services discrimination cases.

The North Carolina Office on the Americans with Disabilities Act shall adopt rules to provide a consistent and comprehensive mechanism for accommodating requests regarding accessibility to public services, and shall adopt dispute resolution procedures to govern responsiveness to those requests. This section does not authorize the North Carolina Office on the Americans with Disabilities Act to adopt rules or procedures that apply to the resolution of matters constituting grounds for a contested case under Chapter 126 of the General Statutes. (2002-163, s. 4.)

§ 168A-11. Civil action.

(a) A person with a disability aggrieved by a discriminatory practice prohibited by G.S. 168A-5 through 168A-8, or a person aggrieved by conduct prohibited by G.S. 168A-10, may bring a civil action to enforce rights granted or protected by this Chapter against any person described in G.S. 168A-5 through 168A-8 or in G.S. 168A-10 who is alleged to have committed such practices or engaged in such conduct. The action shall be commenced in superior court in the county where the alleged discriminatory practice or prohibited conduct occurred or where the plaintiff or defendant resides. Such action shall be tried to the court without a jury.

(b) Any relief granted by the court shall be limited to declaratory and injunctive relief, including orders to hire or reinstate an aggrieved person or admit such person to a labor organization. In a civil action brought to enforce provisions of this Chapter relating to employment, the court may award back pay. Any such back pay liability shall not accrue from a date more than two years prior to the filing of an action under this Chapter. Interim earnings or amounts earnable with reasonable diligence by the aggrieved person shall operate to reduce the back pay otherwise allowable.

(c) No court shall have jurisdiction over an action filed under this Chapter where the plaintiff has commenced federal judicial or administrative proceedings under Section 503 or Section 504 of the Vocational Rehabilitation Act of 1973, 29 U.S.C. §§ 793 and 794, as amended, or federal regulations promulgated under those sections; or under the Americans with Disabilities Act of 1990, 42 U.S.C. § 12101, et seq., as amended, or federal regulations promulgated under that Act, involving or arising out of the facts and circumstances involved in the alleged discriminatory practice under this Chapter. If such proceedings are commenced after a civil action has been commenced under this Chapter, the State court's jurisdiction over the civil action shall end and the action shall be forthwith dismissed.

(d) In any civil action brought under this Chapter, the court, in its discretion, may award reasonable attorney's fees to the substantially prevailing party as part of costs. (1985, c. 571, s. 1; 1999-160, s. 1.)

§ 168A-12. Statute of limitations.

A civil action regarding employment discrimination brought pursuant to this Chapter shall be commenced within 180 days after the date on which the aggrieved person became aware of or, with reasonable diligence, should have become aware of the alleged discriminatory practice or prohibited conduct. A civil action brought pursuant to this Chapter regarding any other complaint of discrimination shall be commenced within two years after the date on which the aggrieved person became aware of or, with reasonable diligence, should have become aware of the alleged discriminatory practice or prohibited conduct. (1985, c. 571, s. 1; 1999-160, s. 1.)

Vision Books Order Form

Fax Orders:	1-704-921-9271
Phone Orders:	1-704-921-9271
E-mail Orders:	www.visionbooks.org
Mail Orders:	Vision Books, LLC P.O. Box 42406 Charlotte, NC 28215

Shipp To:
Name_____
Address_____
City_____State_____Zip_____
Phone_____Fax_____
Email_____@_____

Bill To: We can bill a third party on your behalf.
Name_____
Address_____
City_____State_____Zip_____
Phone___(_____)_____Fax_____
Email_____@_____

Pamphlet Number ($15.00 Each)	Qty	Total Cost
_____	_____	_____
_____	_____	_____
_____	_____	_____
_____	_____	_____
_____	_____	_____
_____	_____	_____
_____	_____	_____
_____	_____	_____
Full Volume Set 1-92	**92 Pamphlets**	**1,380.00**

Free Shipping & Handling on Full Volume Orders
Add $1.00 Shipping & Handling Per Pamphlet $_____

Total Cost $_____

DID YOU ENJOY THIS BOOK?

Vision Books, LLC would like to hear from you! If you or someone you know has been fasely imprisoned, we would like to hear your story. If the 'North Carolina Criminal Law and Procedure' has had an effect in your life or if you have suggestions, we would like to hear from you. Send your letters to:

Vision Books, LLC
Attn: Staff Writers
P.O. Box 42406
Charlotte, NC 28215
Email: staff@visionbooks.org

Order Additional Copies:

Fax Orders:	1-980-299-5965
Phone Orders:	1-704-898-0770
E-mail Orders:	www.visionbooks.org
Mail Orders:	Vision Books, LLC P.O. Box 42406 Charlotte, NC 28215

www.ingramcontent.com/pod-product-compliance
Lightning Source LLC
Chambersburg PA
CBHW071759200526
45167CB00017B/524